EDITOR: MARTIN WIND

OSPREY
MILITARY

MEN-AT-ARMS

GERMAN AIRBORNE
TROOPS 1939-45

Text by
BRUCE QUARRIE
Colour plates by
MIKE CHAPPELL

First published in Great Britain in 1983 by
Osprey Publishing, Elms Court, Chapel Way, Botley,
Oxford OX2 9LP United Kingdom

© Copyright 1983
Osprey Publishing Limited
Reprinted June 1983, 1984, (twice), 1985, 1986, 1987
(twice), 1988, 1989, 1991, 1993, 1994 (twice), 1995,
1996 (twice), 1997, 1998

British Library Cataloguing in Publication Data
Quarrie, Bruce
   German airborne troops 1939–45—(Men-at-Arms
   series; 139)
   1. Germany. *Heer*—Airborne forces
   I. Title   II. Series
   356.1660943   UD485.G/

   ISBN 0–85045–480–8

Filmset in Great Britain
Printed through World Print Ltd., Hong Kong

For a catalogue of all books published by Osprey
Military/Automotive/Aviation please write to:

The Marketing Manager
Osprey Publishing Ltd.
P.O. Box 140
Wellingborough
Northants NN8 4ZA
United Kingdom

Acknowledgements and sources
In writing this book I have received much help from a
wide variety of people. In particular I must thank Hans
Teske, a former paratrooper with FJR 5, for so patiently
answering my many questions and helping in photo
identification; David List for much invaluable help on
unit markings; Andrew Baker, Gavin Cadden, Major F.
O. Finzel, Graham Thompson, Werner Regenberg,
Josef Charita, Fernando J. de Zavalia, Timo Tuominen,
Gordon Williamson, Alfred Otte of the Kamerad-
schaftsbund Fallschirmpanzerkorps, Eckart Brandt, L.
Ferdinand-Fricke, J. Freitas, Larry Horsfield, A. G.
Dixon, Ken Jones, K. J. Hill of the RAC Tank Museum,
Bovington and, in particular, Martin, for his patience.
Sources studied include original documents in the Public
Record Office and the Bundesarchiv, various issues of
Strategy & Tactics, Volkmar Kuhn's *German Paratroops*
(which must be read with care as it contains many
errors), Rudolf Böhmler and Werner Haupt's *Fallschirm-
jäger*, Terry Gander's *Small Arms, Artillery and Special
Weapons of the Third Reich*, Ian Hogg and John Weeks'
Military Smallarms of the Twentieth Century, Major John R.
Angolia's *Insignia of the Third Reich* and Brian L. Davis'
German Parachute Forces 1935–45.

The Fallschirmjäger Role

'Airborne operations have often been called a vertical envelopment, and therein lies one of the best descriptions of their value. The essence of an envelopment is to pin the enemy in place so that he can be destroyed. A strong enemy force to one's rear disrupts supplies and communications and makes one more vulnerable to an attack from the front. It also has a major psychological impact. One of the certainties upon which soldiers rely is that everything to their front is the enemy and everything to their rear is friendly. It helps distinguish who to fire on and who to assume are reinforcements.

'Airborne operations change that. They also force a withdrawal of troops from the main line, first to defend against possible drops on key positions and then to reduce the pockets, if possible, once they are down. In some ways, airborne is impossible to defend against. Unless one guesses exactly right (or has access to the plans), the attacker can usually put a larger force on the ground at a given point than the defender can spare to defend it against drops. It is only when fortune intervenes . . . that paratroopers can be destroyed while dropping, before they can form defensive positions.'[1]

The foregoing quotation is probably the most concisely informative appraisal of airborne operations that I have yet encountered. It states the advantages of this form of attack succinctly whilst making the possible pitfalls unspokenly apparent. Surprise is the keynote, coupled with suitable winds and weather, an objective which can be held until relief arrives, accurate intelligence of enemy forces which can be assembled in the vicinity sufficiently rapidly for an effective counter-attack—and, of course, luck.

To an aggressor the value of airborne troops, used properly, far outweighs their numerical strength. It would almost certainly be false to say that the German invasion of France and the Low Countries in 1940 could not have succeeded without the paratroops and their glider-borne comrades; but it would certainly have been made more difficult.

A Fallschirmjäger NCO gives the order to advance. This photo was probably taken late in the war, as he wears the Luftwaffe camouflaged combat jacket rather than the paratrooper's smock. Note string net helmet cover, another late-war feature; elasticated gauntlets, automatic holster, one set of MP40 pouches, binoculars and stick grenade. (Bündesarchiv 576/1848/32. Please note that all photographs used in this book, unless specifically credited otherwise, are from the Bündesarchiv collection at Koblenz. The serial numbers are quoted for reference purposes; but note that Bündesarchiv cannot fill orders for prints from members of the public.)

[1] 'What good is airborne', Stephen B. Patrick, *Strategy & Tactis* 77.

Hitler congratulates paratroop officers after the Eben Emael operation; left to right are Lt. Meissner, Oblt. Zierach and Hptm. Walter Koch. They display three slightly different models of the early grey-green jump smock, with two breast pockets, one breast pocket, and pockets on breast and thigh. (via Gavin Cadden)

Germany was a late starter in the development of airborne forces, though far in front of Britain, America, or her later ally, Japan. The potential of this new weapon was, surprisingly, first recognised in two of the most militarily backward countries of the world, Italy and the recently-created Soviet Union. The first effective static-line parachute was developed in Italy during the 1920s[2], and Russia demonstrated the military potential of airborne forces in the early '30s.

The early Soviet methods were crude. The troops had to leave their slow-moving ANT-6 aircraft through a hole in the fuselage roof, then gingerly edge their way out along the wings, before jumping together and pulling their rip-cords. This was hardly a safe arrangement, although it did result in

[2]Static-line—i.e. automatically opening—parachutes were essential for massed paratroop operations. Individual rip-cord opening would have required drops from higher altitude, with inevitably greater casualties and worse scattering. Training would also have been more complex and dangerous.

very tight grouping on the dropping zone, especially when one considers that the aircraft had to slow down to 60mph, not far above its stall, in order to make the operation feasible! At such a speed surprise was hardly possible, and the aircraft itself would have been especially vulnerable to ground fire, even from small arms.

However, German military thinkers—excluded under the terms of the Treaty of Versailles from developing modern military forces but, under the Weimar Republic and during the early days of Hitler, enjoying the facility of Russian training grounds and access to manoeuvres—appreciated the flexibility in attack which airborne forces could give, and turned their thoughts to what could be accomplished 'at home'. Perhaps they were thinking of the smiling remark which Red Air Force Marshal Michal Schtscherbakov had made to the French Marshal Petain during a tour of the Maginot Line: 'Fortresses like this may well be superfluous in the future if your potential adversary . . . parachutes over them.'

Be that as it may, German observers to the Russian manoeuvres in 1935 and '36, who had witnessed the parachuting on to a precise objective

Fallschirmjäger MG34 team on an exercise: note temporary red cloth bands worn round the plain grey-green helmet covers.(540/419/19)

of a full regiment of 1,000 troops, followed by the air landing of 5,000 reinforcements, were undeniably impressed. Göring was amongst these and, in March–April 1935, he reconstituted his Landespolizeigruppe 'General Göring' as the first fledgling airborne regiment.[3] This was incorporated into the Luftwaffe on 1 October the same year, and training commenced at Altengrabow. After a demonstration parachute jump during which the jumper injured himself and had to be carried off on a stretcher, sufficient officers and men (600) perhaps surprisingly volunteered for parachute training for the 1st Jäger Battalion, Regiment 'General Göring', to be established in January 1936 under the command of Major, later Colonel, Bruno Bräuer.

At this time Göring and the Luftwaffe were not the only parties interested in the potential of airborne forces, and the Heer (Army), Schutzstaffel (SS) and Sturmabteilung (SA, or 'brownshirts') also became involved. The latter were to disappear in the infamous Röhm putsch, but the SS maintained a tiny parachute arm to the end; the 500th SS Fallschirmjägerbataillon, a penal unit led by

Hauptsturmführer Rybka, distinguished itself during the parachute and glider-borne assault on Tito's mountain headquarters in June 1944. The Army's attempt to retain its own paratroop force was quashed by Göring, who brought all the Wehrmacht Fallschirmjäger under the aegis of the Luftwaffe.

Due partly to the rivalry between the various hierarchies within the Nazi state, as well as to lack of experience, there was considerable confusion as to the future role of a German paratroop force; but this was shortly to be clarified both by the experience of surviving volunteer 'guinea pigs' from the Condor Legion in Spain, and by the appointment of a man who, if Guderian is hailed as the father of the German Panzertruppe, must be given a similar honorific in respect of the Fallschirmjäger: Generalmajor Kurt Student.

The official inauguration of the German paratroop arm dates from an Order of the Day signed by Luftwaffe Reichsminister Milch on Göring's behalf on 29 January 1936. This called for the recruitment

---

[3] See Vanguard 4, *Fallschirmpanzerdivision 'Hermann Göring'*.

The standard transport used for parachute operations was the Junkers Ju52/3m trimotor, the Luftwaffe's versatile old workhorse, which appeared in many different versions. It was used both for parachute drops—accommodating from 12 to 18 paratroopers—and for glider towing. With a cruising speed of around 125mph, it had a range of 600 miles at 18,000 feet.(via Hans Obert)

of volunteers for parachute training at Stendal. The rigorous standard of this training is emphasised by Hitler's own 'ten commandments' to the Fallschirmjäger, the first of which, translated, reads: 'You are the chosen fighting men of the Wehrmacht. You will seek combat and train yourselves to endure all hardships. Battle shall be your fulfilment.' (There was a great deal more in this vein, but it is worth quoting one additional injunction, which characterises Fallschirmjäger operations throughout the war: 'Against an open foe, fight with chivalry, but extend no quarter to a guerrilla.')

The second Fallschirmjäger battalion, also formed in 1936, was an army unit under Major (later Generalleutnant) Richard Heidrich, and was organised like a support battalion with heavy machine guns and mortars. It took part with distinction in the autumn 1937 Wehrmacht manoeuvres at Mecklenburg, and gave greater impetus to the consolidation of the German parachute arm; but quite apart from the continuing haggling between the army and the air force over

jurisdiction, opinion was divided over Fallschirmjäger function. The Luftwaffe at this time believed in a policy of using the paratroops in small units as saboteurs behind enemy lines to disrupt communications and morale, while the army felt they should be used in strength, almost like conventional infantry. In the end, exponents of both viewpoints were to see their ideas tested, and it is to the credit of the Fallschirmjäger and their instructors that they were able to fulfil both expectations.

The next stage in the development of the Luftwaffe's paratroop arm, in July 1938, was the detachment of Bräuer's battalion from the 'General Göring' Regiment to form the nucleus of the new 7.Flieger-Division (7th Airborne Division) under Kurt Student, ably assisted by Majors Gerhard Bassenge and G. Trettner. The general (born 12 May 1890) was admirably suited for such an appointment, having served both as an infantryman and later as a fighter pilot and squadron leader during the First World War and, latterly, as one of the staff officers closely involved with building up Germany's clandestine air force prior to Hitler's accession to power. Unlike many of his contemporaries, Student was both trusted by the Nazi hierarchy and liked by the men under his command. And although a Luftwaffe appointment, he was acceptable to the army because he disagreed with the air force's doctrine of using paratroops in 'penny packets' as saboteurs.

Although the occupation of the Sudetenland in the autumn of 1938 did not require the exercise of military force, Student's new 'division' took part as an exercise. Göring was so enthusiastic that army objections were overridden, and Heidrich's 2. Fallschirmjägerbataillon was amalgamated into the Luftwaffe. At the same time (January 1939), instructions were issued for the raising of a second regiment, and Heidrich's pride was salved by promoting him to command this unit. Both regiments were to be operational by the time of the Norwegian campaign in the spring of the following year. They were organised along standard infantry lines, each regiment comprising three battalions (in 1940 the 2nd Regiment only had two), each battalion being of four companies. A pioneer company was already in existence, and a start had been made on raising the necessary supporting formations such as anti-tank, light field and anti-aircraft artillery, reconnaissance, engineer, signals, medical and other units.

The glider used for combat landings was the DFS230; with a span of 68ft. 5½ins. and a length of 36ft. 10½ins., it could carry eight fully equipped troops, and had a roof hatch mounting for an MG15 machine gun. Once committed to its landing run it presented a large and vulnerable target, unable to take evasive action, and the danger of a crash-landing killing or disabling the troops was obviously quite high. Against these risks, the glider ensured that a section, with all its equipment immediately to hand, landed together.(via Hans Obert)

Fallschirmjäger Operations

The Fallschirmjäger were not committed in any strength to the invasion of Poland, although men of the 7.Flieger-Division are known to have made a probing reconnaissance across the River Vistula, during which they sustained several casualties at Wola Gulowska. General Student reported to Hitler the paratroops' disappointment at not being able to participate in the Polish campaign, to which the latter replied: 'They will certainly see some action in the West!'

Norway and Denmark, 1940

The first operations were in Denmark and Norway, and involved Major Erich Walther's 1 Btl. of Fallschirmjägerregiment Nr 1 (I/FJR 1). His four companies were assigned a difficult task. The HQ and 2nd Companies were to capture Fornebu airfield, Oslo, and hold it until the 163rd Infantry Division could be flown in. The 3rd Company, commanded by Leutnant Freiherr von Brandis, was similarly to secure Sola airfield, Stavanger; while the 4th Company, under Hauptmann Walther Gericke, had one platoon detached to capture two airfields at Aalborg, the remainder being committed to the causeway linking the islands of Falster and Seeland. The 1st Company, under Leutnant Herbert Schmidt, was held in reserve, but

Paratrooper in Russia, wearing a thin snow-camouflage suit over his combat uniform and with his helmet whitewashed. Apart from the holstered automatic and MP40 he is also armed with a Haft-Hohllandung 3kg magnetic anti-tank charge.(555/902/12)

before being forced to surrender when their ammunition ran out. Schmidt himself had been badly wounded in the hip and stomach but retained command throughout the operation, for which he was awarded the Knight's Cross. Despite casualties, therefore, the Scandinavian operations of April 1940 vindicated the use of paratroopers against unprepared opposition when surprise was on their side. But it was in the following month that the Fallschirmjäger were to lay the true foundations of their later reputation.

The West, 1940

For the invasion of France and the Low Countries, Student's 7.Flieger-Division was combined in an ad hoc air group with the 22.Luftlande-Division (ordinary infantry transported by air) under overall command of Kesselring's Luftflotte.2. Their most important single objective was the Belgian fortress of Eben Emael, part of the chain of defences in front of the Albert Canal. Containing 18 artillery pieces in casemates some six feet thick, plus anti-tank and machine gun positions, and actually sunk into the side of the canal itself, Eben Emael could have proved a severe stumbling block to conventional forces, especially since speed was the very essence of blitzkrieg.

After talking over the problem with Bräuer, Student decided to form a special assault group under Hauptmann Walter Koch, a tough 29-year-old who had earlier been in the Prussian security police and the 'General Göring' Regiment. For this task he was allocated his own company from I/FJR 1 plus Leutnant Witzig's pioneer company from II/FJR 1, a total of 11 officers and 427 men. Rigorous training commenced at Hidelsheim, where the men were organised into four assault groups. Only one of these would actually attack Eben Emael, the 85-strong Assault Group 'Granite' under Leutnant Witzig. Assault Group 'Steel' (Leutnant Altmann) had the Veldvezelt bridge as its objective; Assault Group 'Concrete' (Leutnant Schacht), the Vroenhoven bridge; and Assault Group 'Iron' (Leutnant Schächter), the Canne bridge. Following the capture of these points, the assault groups were to hold their objectives until relieved by advancing Wehrmacht columns, notably 4.Panzer-Division. All of these attacks were to be glider-borne, in contrast with the Fallschirm-

later dropped to assist General Dietl's forces around Narvik.

Major Walther encountered bad luck: Fornebu was shrouded in fog, and he was forced to turn back. However, the following waves of Ju52s carrying the men of the 163rd found a break in the cover and landed, suffering many casualties but capturing the airfield. Leutnant von Brandis was more fortunate, his men landing safely on the edge of Sola and quickly overcoming the isolated pockets of resistance so that the back-up troops could land safely. Hauptmann Gericke was even luckier, as the Danish troops guarding the causeway were so shocked at the sight of the Fallschirmjäger that they surrendered without a fight. The single platoon dropped to capture the two Aalborg airfields also succeeded without bloodshed. Leutnant Schmidt's company made a twilight drop into the snow-covered Gudbrandsal valley some 90 miles north of Oslo. They suffered casualties from determined Norwegian defenders during the drop, but continued to fight in appalling conditions for four days jäger operations in Holland the same month, which were all parachute drops.

First on the ground was Assault Group 'Concrete', at 0515 on the morning of 10 May 1940. They came under heavy fire during their approach and were hard pressed by the Belgian defenders for the remainder of the day, being able to retire at 2140 only after relief by a Wehrmacht infantry battalion.

Assault Groups 'Steel' and 'Granite' landed practically simultaneously at 0520. In the attack on the Veldvezelt bridge Leutnant Altmann discovered that the Belgian demolition charges had been removed, and the objective was reported as in his hands by 1535. This turned out to be premature, as his men had to beat off several counter-attacks during the day until relieved at 2130.

In Eben Emael the Belgian defenders had been alerted at 0030 by reports of German troop movements, but they believed themselves safe behind the front lines. Witzig's Assault Group 'Granite' paraded at 0330 and precisely an hour later their 11 glider-tugs took off, the pioneers laden down with satchels of explosives. At 0520 they were over their objective and the gliders cast loose to drift menacingly down through the still dawn air. The Belgians were stupefied—nothing had prepared them for this—and they did not open fire until the DFS230 gliders were almost on the ground.

The landing was a good one, even though two gliders—including that carrying Leutnant Witzig—had had to abort. However, the attack (now commanded by Oberfeldwebel Wenzel) went ahead without a hitch. Even before the gliders had slid to a halt their doors were flung open and the Fallschirmjäger debouched, rushing into the assault with their flamethrowers and hollow-charge demolition devices under covering machine gun fire from the top hatches of the DFS230s. Within minutes seven casemates and 14 Belgian guns were out of action, and the attackers were inside the fort. At 0540 Wenzel radioed Koch: 'Reached objective. Everything going to plan.' However, the greater part of the fort was still in Belgian hands.

At 0830 Leutnant Witzig, who had organised a fresh tow for his glider, landed alongside his men and resumed charge of the operation. Despite the paratroopers' initial success, however, the Belgians began to rally; the attackers were forced to take shelter in the captured casemates, where they sat out the night of 10/11 May until reinforced by an engineer battalion in the morning. The new arrivals spurred the Fallschirmjäger on to even greater efforts and it was not long before a white flag fluttered from a Belgian strongpoint.

From every viewpoint the attack on Eben Emael had been a tremendous German victory. Of Witzig's original 85 officers and men, only six had been killed (although 20 were wounded). The surprise of the attack had crippled Belgian morale—even though there were over 1,000 men in the fort—and, as Kurt Student said later, it was 'a deed of exemplary daring and decisive significance'.

The last party, Assault Group 'Iron', was unlucky. A German mechanised column had advanced ahead of its schedule, with the result that the Canne bridge was demolished by the Belgian defenders, and the glider-borne Fallschirmjäger

This Oberleutnant wears the wings-and-bars sleeve ranking patches, copied by the Fallschirmjäger from their colleagues in the Luftwaffe's aircrew branch. For details of this outfit see Plate G.(553/839/27)

Fallschirmjäger sentry beside a Russian railway track. He wears the 'second pattern Luftwaffe' smock, of grey-green but with button-in 'legs'; and note details of gravity knife pocket on the outside of the right trouser leg.(541/432/15)

The general plan was to use the Fallschirmjäger to seize important river crossings and airfields inside Holland, as in previous operations, but to combine this with a major street-fighting attack by the 22nd Air-Landing Division to capture the Hague and neutralise the Dutch high command. The main paratroop objectives were the Moerdyk and Dordrecht bridges, plus Waalhaven and Valkenburg airfields. I and II/FJR 1 were assigned the first two tasks; III/FJR 1 the third; and six companies of FJR 2 plus the 47th Infantry Regiment (which, with the 16th and 65th, made up Graf von Sponeck's 22nd Division), Valkenburg.

First under fire on 10 May was Hauptmann Karl-Lothar Schulz's III/FJR 1 at Waalhaven, whose capture was essential if the remainder of von Sponeck's division was to land intact. The airfield, like other Dutch objectives, was heavily bombed before the assault, but the paras nevertheless came under heavy machine gun fire as they landed. Determinedly they stormed the airport buildings—where the Dutch commander had been celebrating his 40th year of service—and took control. Messerschmitt Bf109s took care of British Hurricanes which tried to interfere with the subsequent landing of the 22nd Division's Ju52s, but a solitary Dutch anti-aircraft battery courageously continued to fire until 'taken out' by the German paras. Once this small but bloody battle was over, the Fallschirmjäger and their reinforcements were able to secure the approach to Rotterdam.

At the other airfield, Valkenburg, FJR 2's six companies had dropped successfully in advance of Von Sponeck's 47th Infantry Regiment; but the surface proved too soft to take the Ju52s, and rapidly became congested. Moreover, the Dutch fought back stubbornly and the Germans were forced on to the defensive; this part of the attack on The Hague had to be abandoned.

The battalions assigned to the capture of the vital Moerdyk and Dordrecht bridges, jumping from both north and south to envelop their objectives, were luckier, although Leutnant Freiherr von Brandis (who had captured Sola airfield during the Norwegian operation) was killed. The Moerdyk bridge was captured with speed and precision, and held until the men of Hauptmann Prager's II/FJR 1 were relieved by 9.Panzer-Division three days later. At 1730 a day later Student, who had flown

had to land in a hail of fire. Schächter was killed and his place taken by Leutnant Joachim Meissner, who held out through two major counter-attacks until relieved at 2330 on the 10th.

In a sense, the operations in Belgium had been an example of Luftwaffe use of paratroops in 'penny packets', and it is worthwhile contrasting them with Fallschirmjäger deployment in Holland. Koch's group comprised fewer than 500 men; four times that number were used against 'Fortress Holland', plus the whole of the 22nd Air-Landing Division under Generalmajor Graf von Sponeck.

Useful photo showing the splinter-camouflaged jump smock in some detail. These men are parading somewhere in the Mediterranean theatre, and have helmets camouflaged in a softly-sprayed sand and grey or green finish. The nearest wears the Spanish Cross decoration, indicating previous service with the Condor Legion. (580/1995/29)

command of the 7.Flieger-Division passed to General Richard Putzier, who had been in charge of the transport arrangements during the operations in the Low Countries. As a result of the paratroopers' successes, the division was enlarged by the creation of a third regiment, FJR 3; and by the expansion of Koch's Assault Group into an assault regiment (Fallschirmjäger-Sturmregiment) of four battalions, commanded by Oberst Eugen Meindl. All this was in preparation for Operation *Seelöwe* (Sealion), the planned invasion of Britain.

Seelöwe was eventually called off, and the next Fallschirmjäger operations were to take place in the warmer climes of the Mediterranean. Student had recovered sufficiently well by January 1941 to resume overall command of German airborne forces: these now comprised the three regiments of the 7.Flieger-Division, the 22nd Air-Landing Division and the Sturmregiment (FJStR), referred to collectively as Fliegerkorps XI.

Greece, 1941

During the Greek campaign FJR 2, which had been operating in Bulgaria, was ordered to prepare to administer a severe shock the Empire Expeditionary Force under General Maitland Wilson. Greek forces in the north, who had earlier delivered a sharp check to Mussolini's troops, had finally been forced to surrender to Il Duce's German allies, and Wilson's forces were retreating towards the Peloponnese. Their only route lay across the narrow neck of land west of Athens divided by the deep Corinth Canal, and it was FJR 2's task to block this. Unfortunately for the Fallschirmjäger, the attack went in a couple of days late; and although a great tactical success, resulting in over 2,000 British and Greek PoWs, it was not the sweeping victory it might have been, since most of the Expeditionary Force escaped by sea.

The operation began at 0500 on the morning of 26 April 1941 when a platoon of II/FJR 2's 6th Company, under Leutnant Hans Teusen, boarded their gliders at Larissa. Their objective was the vital bridge across the canal. Two hours later they landed under heavy fire, but rapidly succeeded in removing most of the demolition charges which had been laid by the British. Then fate took a hand; a stray shell from a Bofors gun exploded the stacked

into Waalhaven shortly after its capture, was able to receive the glad news of a similar feat at Dordrecht. The Dutch troops had, by and large, fought better than their Belgian counterparts, but surprise and local numerical superiority had been on the side of the Fallschirmjäger. On 14 May the Netherlands surrendered. Unfortunately, in a bizarre footnote to the operation, Student himself was seriously wounded in the head by SS troops engaged in disarming Dutch soldiers.

While Student was fighting for his life in hospital,

charges, demolishing the bridge and killing many of Teusen's men. The balance of II/FJR 2 landed shortly afterwards, however, and took off southwards in pursuit of the retreating British. Although grossly outnumbered, Teusen persuaded the British officer in charge that his men were the vanguard of an entire division, supported by Stukas, and accepted their surrender. For this daring act Teusen—who had continued to fight although wounded—was awarded the Knight's Cross.

Crete, 1941

What followed next has entered airborne legend: the invasion of Crete. But Student's long-term strategic plans for follow-up operations against the northern end of the Suez Canal, Alexandria and Malta were never pursued (any more than an earlier plan for the airborne invasion of Gibraltar at the time when *Seelöwe* fell through), and this makes the operation doubly unique: it succeeded, but under circumstances which prevented its planned exploitation.

Student had proposed to the OKL on 20 April 1941 that the conquest of Crete was a necessary supplement to the Balkan campaign, since British airfields on the island brought the vital Ploesti

oilfields within their range. Göring acceded, and so in the end did Hitler, although the Wehrmacht wanted to use the Fallschirmjäger against Malta first.

Meanwhile, the organisation within Fliegerkorps XI had altered. The 22nd Air-Landing Division had been diverted specifically to guard the Ploesti oilfields, and in its place Student had Generalmajor Ringel's 5th Mountain Division. His forces for Operation *Merkur*—the airborne invasion of Crete—were thus as follows on 20 May 1941:

First, the renamed Luftlande-Sturm-Regiment (ex-Fallschirmjäger-Sturmregiment) under Generalmajor Meindl (I/LLStR, Major Koch; II/LLStR, Major Stentzler; III/LLStR, Major Scherber; and IV/LLStR, Hauptmann Gericke).

Second, 7.Flieger-Division under Generalleutnant Süssmann, comprising: FJR 1 under Oberst Bräuer (I/FJR 1 Major Walther; II/FJR 1 Hauptmann Burckhardt; and III/FJR 1, Major Schulz); FJR 2 under Oberst Alfred Sturm I/FJR 2, Major Kroh; II/FJR 2, Hauptmann Pietzonka; and III/FJR 2, Hauptmann Wiedemann); and FJR 3 under Oberst Heidrich: (I/FJR 3, Hauptmann Freiherr von der Heydte; II/FJR 3, Major Derpa; and III/FJR 3, Major Heilmann).

Third, 5. Gebirgs-Division under Generalmajor Ringel, comprising: Gebirgsjäger-Regiment 85 unter Oberst Krakau (I/GJR 85, Major Dr Treck; II/GJR 85, Major Esch; and III/GJR 85, Major Fett); Gebirgsjäger-Regiment 100 under Oberst Utz (I/GJR 100, Major Schrank; II/GJR 100, Major Friedmann; and III/GJR 100, Major Ehall); Gebirgs-Artillerie-Regiment 95 under Oberstleutnant Wittmann (I/GArtR 95, Major von Sternbach, and II/GArtR 95, Major Raithel); plus the 95th Mountain Motor-Cycle, Pioneer, Anti-Tank and Reconnaissance Battalions under Majors Nolte, Schätte, Bindermann and Graf Castell zu Castell respectively.

In addition to these forces, Fliegerkorps XI's Corps troops included a light flak battalion, while 7.Flieger's divisional troops included pioneer, artillery, machine gun and anti-tank battalions.

The plan for the capture of the island as eventually evolved called for these forces to be dropped in two phases on four main objectives, three of which were airfields. The first objective fell to Meindl's Assault Regiment, and comprised the

Probably a posed shot taken in Crete after the fighting of May 1941, to guess from the sand-camouflaged helmets and early grey-green jump smocks. The Feldwebel at left has his blouse collar outside his smock, to display ranking, and does not wear sleeve patches: these seem to have been rather slow and uneven in issue.(569/1579/15)

airfield at Maleme plus the capture of various roads, bridges and anti-aircraft positions in the Canea region, with help from Heidrich's FJR 3. This was the first wave. In the second wave, Sturm's FJR 2 was to capture the airfield and town of Rethymnon (Retimo), while Bräuer's FJR 1 was rather out on a limb some miles down the coast, attacking the airfield and town of Heraklion. Ringel's 5th Mountain Division was to be brought in by air to support these operations as the capture of airfields permitted. In this event, German intelligence was proved faulty, and things did not go off exactly as planned.

To begin with, Admiral Canaris' Abwehr had mistakenly thought that most of the 50,000-plus troops evacuated from Greece had been shipped straight to Egypt; this was not true. Secondly, it was not appreciated that the British garrison had not only had time to prepare, but was also alerted to the fact that the main assault would be airborne. And thirdly, it was not known that General Bernard Freyberg, the much-decorated and highly aggressive New Zealand commander of the Allied Forces on Crete, had accurately forecast the main German landing areas and prepared accordingly, with 'booby traps' for both parachutists and gliders.

Nor was this all. The German invaders expected to meet only British and Greek troops who had been thoroughly demoralised by their defeat on the mainland. In this overconfidence they were to be fatally mistaken.

Nevertheless, although anticipated, the basic attack plan was sound, aiming as it did at the two operational airfields of Maleme and Heraklion, the limited landing ground at Rethymnon, and General Freyberg's supposed headquarters and main garrison at Canea.

Maleme lies in the north-east corner of Crete, in a rugged terrain of olive groves. Today it is an attractive tourist centre; but on 20 May 1941 it was a parched, dusty hell for both the Fallschirmjäger and the stubborn British defenders. Although the airfield runway was only some 600 metres in length, its capture was vital to the success of the operation; and a necessary prelude to this was the elimination of the well dug-in and camouflaged British anti-aircraft positions. Following a Stuka attack, the LLStR's vanguard—one company of 90 men under Leutnant Genz—landed their DFS230 gliders in a

From the same sequence: the top hatch gunner of a DFS230 glider manning an MG15.(568/1529/28)

hail of fire at approximately 0700. Despite heavy casualties, they succeeded in knocking out the AA positions south of the airfield. They were followed by the remainder of the I/LLStR, commanded by Major Koch, whose orders were to consolidate and then launch an assault on the airfield itself. The battalion's 3rd Company landed as planned, but the 4th and HQ Companies went off course and landed in the middle of a strong British position. Major Koch was wounded within minutes, along with over half his men. The planned assault was obviously impossible under these conditions. However, the 3rd Company, which had landed on the western perimeter of the airfield, was able to dig itself into a dried-up river bed and, supported by survivors from other units who gradually joined up during the morning, they eventually succeeded in subduing the western and southern perimeter defences.

III/LLStR dropped by parachute in the area to the north-east of the airfield, but the men were scattered and initially unable to consolidate, especially since they—like the 1st Battalion—came under steady and heavy fire from a hill known as Point 107. The HQ and 4th Battalion successfully landed in the vicinity of a large bridge to the west of the airfield; but Generalmajor Meindl was seriously wounded, and tactical command of the regiment was assumed by Major Stentzler, CO of the 2nd Battalion, which had been intended as the regiment's reserve. By the evening of the first day the Assault Regiment had therefore invested but

A bearded paratrooper in the desert. He wears the sand-coloured Luftwaffe tropical tunic, a splinter-camouflaged helmet cover, and a blue-grey rifle bandolier; sun-and-sand goggles are slung round his neck.(550/761/4a)

not secured the airfield, while a counter-attack was expected at any moment, leading to a sleepless night for the battle-weary Fallschirmjäger.

Oberst Heidrich's FJR 3 landed to the west of the LLStR's objective, its task being to capture Galatas, Canea and Suda Bay.

In the vanguard was Major Heilmann's 3rd Battalion, which parachuted into the middle of a surprised but determined force of New Zealanders. Only one company—the 9th—landed in the right place, the others landing respectively in the mountains, in a reservoir where most were drowned, and in the middle of a New Zealand camp where they were quickly captured. After fighting all day to hold a hill outside Galatas, the much-depleted 9th Company was forced to withdraw.

FJR 3's 1st Battalion dropped near the Agya prison, a useful strongpoint from which they could control the Alikianon–Canea road. They landed near their target but immediately came under

heavy machine gun fire—watched from a nearby country house by King George II of Greece, who beat a hasty but unnoticed retreat to Alikianon! Accompanied by the 2nd Battalion, I/FJR 3 succeeded in securing the prison and turning it into regimental headquarters, but they were unable to make any headway towards Canea. Heilmann's 3rd Battalion joined up with them that evening.

Practically everything had gone wrong for the first wave. None of their prime objectives had been secured and several battalion and company commanders had been killed; the divisional commander himself, Generalleutnant Süssmann, lay dead in his crashed glider, while Generalmajor Meindl was seriously wounded. Back on the Greek mainland, however, nothing of this was known. But the second wave had its own problems. The time allowed for reloading the returning transport aircraft was too short, as they had to be refuelled by hand from jerrycans in sweltering heat; and the constant activity had stirred up huge dust clouds which further slowed down operations. The aircraft of the second wave were therefore forced to take off and fly in small groups rather than en masse.

FJR 2 took off for Rethymnon at 1330, minus its 2nd Battalion which had been assigned Heraklion as its target. Two companies dropped in the right place but were immediately pinned down by heavy fire, while the third landed some five miles away on rocky ground which resulted in many injuries. Nevertheless, the companies succeeded in consolidating and capturing the vineyard-covered hill overlooking Rethymnon airfield. It was impossible to take the field itself so the paras dug in for the night.

FJR 1, reinforced by the II/FJR 2, took off after the latter force, its objective the third airfield at Heraklion. The area was heavily defended, forcing the Ju52s to fly higher than usual, and as a result many of Bräuer's men were machine-gunned during their descent. Two companies which landed on the western edge of the airfield were wiped out almost to a man (there were only five survivors, who escaped by swimming down the coast). Other units were widely dispersed, and Bräuer had to abandon any idea of taking the airfield on the first day; indeed, it was to take him all night to bring his scattered forces together.

At the end of the first day the situation looked

bleak to the survivors of the 7,000 Fallschirmjäger who had set out in such high spirits, and the only reason General Student persevered with the operation was because he would otherwise have had to abandon his men. Fortunately for the men marooned on Crete, General Freyberg did not counter-attack in strength during the night. Instead, only local and limited counter-attacks were launched, and these the paratroopers were able to repel. Thus, although the battle for Crete still hung in the balance, the Allies lost their best opportunity of sweeping the Germans into the sea—with disastrous results.

Back at Maleme, I/LLStR again attacked Point 107 during the early hours of 21 May, this time successfully. Two anti-aircraft guns were captured and immediately turned to shooting up targets on the airfield. Amazingly, a solitary Ju52 now succeeded in landing on the field without being shot to pieces; crates of ammunition were passed out, the seriously wounded bundled inside, and the pilot nonchalantly took off again! This was followed by a German air strike; but to the paratroopers' surprise the enemy remained remarkably quiescent, making no attempt at a counter-attack.

In III/LLStR's area the scene was one of carnage as dawn broke, for Cretan partisans had mutilated all the dead and wounded they could find during the hours of darkness. Fallschirmjäger reprisals were to be harsh, as one sequence of photographs in the German archives at Koblenz clearly illustrate. (The German authorities have never permitted the author to obtain prints of these particular negatives.) At least 135 Fallschirmjäger are known to have been killed by partisans from this battalion's initial strength of 580 and their bodies have never been recovered.

At 1400 on the 21st a renewed aerial bombardment of Maleme was immediately followed by the landing of the LLStR's remaining two companies, and with their help the airfield defences were finally overrun after a hard fight. Shortly afterwards Oberst Bernhard Ramcke landed with an additional 550 men, in front of the first wave of Ringel's mountain troops. GJR 100 was first to emplane, at 1500, and cheers rang out from the weary Fallschirmjäger as the first ungainly Ju52 touched down at Maleme. But triumph soon turned to chaos, as the tiny airfield was not designed to

Gen. Ramcke, his exact rank at this date obscured in this photo, decorates a paratrooper NCO somewhere in the Mediterranean theatre. They both wear tropical uniform, the NCO with shirtsleeves and shorts and Ramcke with tunic and slacks. The general retains his gold-piped blue-grey side-cap.(166/521/19)

cope with such a large volume of traffic; aircraft collided with each other, littering the perimeter with their wreckage as they were hastily hauled clear of the runway.

Whatever the confusion at Maleme, it was better than the fate which had overtaken GJR 100's 3rd Battalion and the 2nd Battalion of GJR 85, which had set sail the previous night in two convoys of small commandeered fishing craft with only the old Italian destroyers *Lupo* and *Sagitario* as escorts. Both convoys were intercepted by British warships and sent to the bottom. Revenge came too late for the Gebirgstruppe when Stukas sank two cruisers and a destroyer the following morning, as well as damaging two battleships and two more cruisers. One officer and 51 men were the only survivors of the two battalions. However, the worst phase of the battle for Crete was now over for the Germans.

The reinforced LLStR quickly consolidated its

hold on the area around Maleme during the afternoon of the 21st and began pushing towards Canea, although they were not to break into the town until the 27th, so stiff was the opposition. At this juncture the mountain troops were ordered to force march to Rethymnon, where their help was urgently needed.

Here, FJR 2 had been pushed out of their vineyard early on the morning of the 21st by a determined Australian assault which forced them back to the protection of an olive oil factory a mile away. For the next four days the Fallschirmjäger held on in the face of heavy artillery bombardments and repeated attacks, some supported by armour. They were two battalions against nearly 7,000 Allied soldiers, and the unequal struggle could not continue. On the night of 25/26 May the 250 survivors slipped under cover of darkness towards Heraklion. However, they were halted the following evening and ordered to establish a defensive position so as to pin down the enemy. The

Australians breached this position on the 28th, but were thrown back by a desperate and costly counter-attack.

On the 29th FJR 2, heartened by reports that the enemy appeared to be falling back and strengthened by supplies parachuted to them from Ju52s, began moving back in the direction of Rethymnon airfield, where the Australians had now established defensive positions around the oil factory. Just as the regiment was advancing to attack early on the morning of the 30th, relief at last arrived in the shape of GJR 85, which had force-marched from Canea and had already taken the factory, along with 1,200 Australian prisoners.

Meanwhile, at the third airfield, Heraklion, Braüer's FJR 1 had succeeded in consolidating during the night of 20/21 May and, in the morning, started moving towards their objective. Unknown to them, they were faced by over 8,000 defenders with ample artillery, and the attack rapidly ground to a halt. The following day FJR 1 rejected an invitation to surrender, and shortly afterwards received a welcome message from HQ telling them that the attack on Heraklion airfield

Fallschirmjäger motorcyclists of a reconnaissance unit in Tunisia, winter 1942/43; all wear the standard continental-issue motorcyclist's proofed coat.(549/742/17)

had been called off, and that they were simply to establish a defensive position to prevent the Allies sending reinforcements westward to Rethymnon. Before they could do this satisfactorily, however, the enemy artillery positions on a hill known as Point 491 had to be eliminated. During that night Schulz's III/FJR 1 worked their way quietly up the hillside and stormed the position. The British gunners were surprised and quickly gave in.

During the 24th Bräuer consolidated his defensive lines, being reinforced on the 25th by an extra battalion dropped by air. The following day the regiment advanced and successfully attacked the hill known as Point 296 which overlooked Heraklion airfield itself. All was set for an attack on the field on the 27th when elements of 5.Gebirgs-Division began to arrive. By this time the Allies were so demoralised that only a small rearguard was left as a forlorn hope to defend the field. In essence, it was the end. That same day General Freyberg ordered evacuation, and the Allied forces began slipping away to the south of the island. Although pursued, and losing 10,000 prisoners to the Gebirgs-jäger, Freyberg succeeded in evacuating some 17,000 men from Sfakia.

Operation *Merkur* had succeeded, but it had been costly. Out of a total force of 22,000 men employed in the invasion, the Germans lost 3,250 dead and missing and 3,400 wounded. Allied losses in dead and wounded were around 2,500, although they lost five times this number as prisoners. Shortly afterwards, Hitler remarked to Student: 'Crete has shown that the days of the paratrooper are finished.' Henceforth they would fight as regular infantry alongside the Wehrmacht.

Ground Operations

Crete was the last major German airborne operation of the war; never again did the Wehrmacht have the necessary resources of men and—particularly—of aircraft, or face the tactical situation to justify such an effort. It was not altogether the final drop of the Fallschirmjäger, however: combat drops by battalion-sized forces on key objectives did recur. In June 1941 paratroops assisted the Brandenburgers to take Russian bridges over the River Dvina. In September 1943 Otto Skorzeny's commandos rescued Mussolini from his Gran Sasso prison in a daring air-landing operation; and in May 1944 the SS parachute penal battalion made a parachute and glider assault on Tito's headquarters at Drvar. As late as the winter of 1944–45 small-scale operations were mounted, by elements of FJR 6 during the Ardennes offensive, and on the Eastern Front to reinforce the defenders of Breslau. In general, however, the Fallschirmjäger fought as elite infantry in the conventional operations of the Wehrmacht; and the author has preferred to devote most of his available space to the truly airborne operations of the first years of the war. The following is intended purely as a summary of deployment.

The mauled 7.Flieger-Division was rebuilt, and in September 1941 II/LLStR led the division to Russia, where it fought on the Leningrad front until March 1943. It was retitled 1.Fallschirmjäger-Division in October 1942. In March 1943 it was withdrawn to the south of France to recover from the heavy casualties suffered in Russia.

Africa

During 1942 the parachute arm was expanded, and was able to provide ad hoc formations for service in North Africa. In mid-July 1942 Generalmajor Ramcke arrived in Africa with his staff, soon to be followed by the rest of his 'Fallschirmjäger-Brigade Ramcke'. The brigade fielded four rifle battalions (I, Maj. Kroh; II, Maj. von der Heydte; III, Maj. Hübner, and IV Fallschirmjäger-Lehr-Bataillon, Maj. Burkhardt) with an artillery battalion and anti-tank and pioneer companies. Arriving by air without transport of its own, it was forced to share the vehicles of Flak-Regiment 135. The brigade was placed in the front line on the Alamein front, in a southern sector between the Italian 'Bologna' and 'Brescia' Divisions. After a limited attack during the battle of Alam el Halfa, the brigade was engaged in heavy defensive fighting during the battle of El Alamein. Written off as lost when Panzerarmee Afrika fell back in the face of Montgomery's breakthrough, 600 men of the brigade performed an astonishing fighting withdrawal across open desert, capturing British transport and driving in to rejoin Rommel's forces near Fuka after crossing 200 miles of enemy-dominated wilderness.

Fallschirmjäger were also heavily committed to the fighting in Tunisia. In November 1942 FJR 5 was flown from Naples to El Aouina airport, Tunis; this was a unit of unblooded volunteers built around a cadre from the Luftlande-Sturm-Regiment and commanded by Oberstleutnant Koch. Another ad hoc unit was the 'Barenthin-Regiment', named after its commander Oberst Walther Barenthin and formed from drafts of paratroopers from various units. The assault pioneers of Witzig's Pioniere-Bataillon 21 were also sent to Tunisia. These units, alongside Ramcke's brigade, fought with great determination against the closing jaws of the Anglo-American forces at Mateur, Medjez-el-Bab and Tebourba, before being captured with the remainder of the Axis forces in Africa early in May 1943.

One incident which has not been related elsewhere deserves a mention, as it indicates that even under conditions very different from those of their early victories the Fallschirmjäger continued to display qualities which won the respect of their enemies. At Depienne in Tunisia in November 1942 'Green Devil' met 'Red Devil' for the first time. Major John Frost—in 1944 the hero of Arnhem

Bridge—commanded the British 2nd Parachute Bn. of 6th Parachute Bde., tasked with the capture of three airfields in the area. Several paras were injured in the drop on to sun-baked ground; since they could not march they were left in the shelter of a nearby building. There they were found by I/FJR 5, who stormed the building in a hail of fire and took the surviving British paras prisoner. The Fallschirmjäger treated their counterparts with great decency, giving them medical aid, food, drink and tobacco before handing them over to another unit and pressing on.

Whether the guard unit was the 19th Reconnaissance Company of 10.Panzer-Division; the Italian 557th SP Artillery Group; the 3rd Company, 1st Bn., Italian 92nd Infantry Regt., or a mixture of men from all three, has never been established. What is certain is that a German officer in command gave orders for the British prisoners to be dragged up against a wall, and that an Italian machine gun crew were ordered to murder them.

At that moment, as if warned by a premonition, Oberstleutnant Walter Koch returned to the scene. He enforced the release and proper treatment of the prisoners, and they eventually found themselves in PoW camps in Italy. Koch himself suffered a severe head wound shortly thereafter; and while convalescing in Germany the hero of Eben Emael died in a mysterious road accident. Surviving members of his regiment attribute this to Gestapo revenge for refusing to observe the Führer's directive designating enemy parachutists as saboteurs who were to be summarily executed.

Italy

In spring 1943 the 2.Fallschirmjäger-Division was formed in France under the command of the newly-promoted Generalleutnant Ramcke. It comprised FJR 2, and the newly-raised FJR 6 and 7, the former drawn partly from IV/LLStR. The division contained various surviving remnants of units which had fought in Africa.

The paratroopers of FJR 3 from 1.FJD fought in Sicily in August 1943, and were successfully withdrawn to the mainland. Both FJR 3 and 4 of this division were soon in action again against the Salerno landings, and the premier parachute formation continued to give a notably good account of itself as it fell back up the Italian mainland. While

Depienne, Tunisia, November 1943: Cpl. Gavin Cadden, right, was one of the men detailed to protect the British wounded in the incident described in the text. At left is Hauptmann Hans Jungwirt of I/FJR 5, wearing the 'Meyer' cap with added cords.(via Gavin Cadden)

Maj.Walter Koch, seen in this rather battered snapshot with his head bandaged after being wounded in Tunisia shortly after intervening to save 2 Para's wounded from being murdered. He wears the four-pocket service tunic; the down-turned tail of the breast eagle was an early-war style.(via Gavin Cadden)

they were fighting before Salerno in September the Badoglio regime toppled Mussolini and declared an armistice with the Allies; 2.FJD was at once flown from southern France to Rome to assist in disarming the Italian forces and stabilising the situation. Walther Gericke, now commanding II/FJR 6, added to his already tough reputation by parachuting with a task force on to Monte Rotondo in an attempt to capture the Italian general staff—an operation which preceded by a few days the Skorzeny mission to the Gran Sasso, involving 90 men drawn from the Waffen-SS and the Fallschirm-Lehr-Bataillon; and another small air drop on the island of Elba by III/FJR 7 on 17 September. On 12/13 November I/FJR 2 dropped on Leros in the Aegean.

During the last months of 1943, 1.FJD continued to fight doggedly on the defensive in Italy. In November/December 2.FJD was sent to the southern Ukraine, fighting there until April 1944. A new 3.FJD was formed in France in October 1943, comprising FJR 5, 8 and 9. A new 4.FJD was formed in December in the Perugia area, comprising FJR 10, 11 and 12; this formation included a cadre from 2.FJD, and former members of the Italian 'Folgore' and 'Nembo' Divisions. Of the two new divisions 3.FJD remained in France, while 4.FJD was thrown into battle against the Anzio landings in January 1944. The parachute divisions were now divided into two new major formations: I. and II.Fallschirm-Korps. The first comprised 1. and 4.FJD, the second 2. and 3.FJD.

If Crete was the epic parachute attack, then Cassino was undoubtedly the epic defence by parachute troops. Dominating Route 6 from the south to Rome, this bastion of the German 'Gustav Line' at the confluence of the Liri, Rapido and Garigliano Rivers in the Liri Valley withstood repeated Allied assaults between mid-January and mid-May 1944. The Fallschirmjäger of 1.FJD (commanded by Generalleutnant Richard Heidrich since Student's promotion to overall command of the two Parachute Corps) burrowed into the increasingly shell-ploughed rubble of the town, and the monastery on the hill above it; and there they stayed. Neither massive artillery bombardment, heavy air raids, nor direct infantry assault ever dislodged the stubborn defenders. As each storm of explosive ceased, the paratroopers would crawl out of their shelters among the pulverised ruins and man their machine gun nests once more, in time to wreak carnage on the Allied infantry painfully exposed on the slopes below. In the end sheer weight of numbers and ordnance allowed the Allies to turn the flank of the Cassino position; but even then, under the guns of the Poles who eventually planted their flag on Monte Cassino, most of the survivors of 1.FJD managed to pull out in good order and escape.

The Last Year

When the Allies landed in Normandy in June 1944 German parachute formations were among the first to be committed. FJR 6 from 2.FJD was early in action against the two US Airborne divisions, being attached to 91.Luftlande-Division of the German Army around Carentan. The remainder of 2.FJD, refitted in Germany in April after

Generaloberst Stumpff, in the white Luftwaffe officer's summer uniform, examines a 3.7cm. anti-tank gun in use by a paratroop unit. The officer at left wears the Fliegerbluse and grey-green jump trousers; Stumpff's aide is in full service dress.(543/562/20)

returning from Russia and now based in Brittany, was entrusted with the defence of Brest; Ramcke held out until 20 September, when the US troops had got within 100 yards of his command post.

Meindl's II.Fallschirm-Korps now comprised 3.FJD and the new 5.FJD, the latter formed near Rheims in March 1944 and consisting of FJR 13, 14 and 15. Both formations were heavily engaged in the St. Lô and Caen sectors, and suffered severe casualties; the 3rd Division was virtually destroyed at Falaise.

Early in September 1944 Student was given command of the impressively-titled '1st Parachute Army', which was entrusted with holding the front in the Low Countries between Antwerp and Maastricht, a distance of some 60 miles. In fact this force of 30,000 men was of very mixed quality. The old standards for airborne volunteers had long been forgotten; new formations were airborne in name only, and were largely filled out with remnants of

Luftwaffe Field Divisions, ground crews who no longer had any bombers to service, and anyone else in Air Force uniform who could hold a rifle, gathered around a small nucleus of veterans drafted from older divisions. Surprisingly, a number of these ad hoc divisions fought with some distinction in the last months of the war.

FJR 6, only survivors of the old 2.FJD, fought against the Allied landings in the Arnhem corridor during Operation 'Market Garden' in September 1944, as did elements of the two divisions mauled in Normandy, 3. and 5.FJD, which were at that time being rebuilt in the Low Countries. More fully reconstituted, the two divisions fought in the Ardennes offensive of December 1944, suffering heavy casualties yet again. FJR 6, led by Freiherr von der Heydte, mounted a small-scale parachute drop in support of the Ardennes attack; on the night of 15 December they dropped in deep snow near the Malmedy-Eupen road, in an attempt to deny the Allies this route for lateral reinforcement on the northern flank of 6th SS Panzer Army's penetration. Only 125 men landed near the target, and their mission was hopeless; von der Heydte was captured a week later.

The fortunes of the Fallschirmjäger in the final stage of the war can best be summarised by a listing of the various formations—although it must be borne in mind that 'divisional' status was often given on paper to small battle-groups:

1.FJD Fought on in Italy until the end, finally surrendering near Imola, April 1945.

2.FJD After the fall of Brest a new '2.FJD' was raised in Holland in December 1944, consisting of a new FJR 2 and 7, and FJR 21. It was destroyed in the Ruhr in spring 1945.

3.FJD After destruction in Normandy, re-formed in Belgium late in 1944 from various Luftwaffe elements; fought under 15th Army in the Ardennes, December 1944; remnant surrendered in the Ruhr, April 1945.

4.FJD Fought on in Italy until final surrender in April 1945 near Vicenza.

5.FJD After heavy losses suffered while fighting in Normandy, rebuilt from various Luftwaffe personnel in France and the Low Countries. Further heavy losses while fighting on southern flank of Ardennes offensive under 7th Army; surrendered in March 1945 near Nürburgring.

6.FJD A 'scratch' formation consisting of FJR 17 and 18, formed in France in June 1944 and effectively destroyed in Normandy, remnants being drafted into 7.FJD. Raised a second time in Holland, and captured by British near Zutphen early in 1945.

7.FJD Designation of an ad hoc collection of units of Luftwaffe ground troops formed into a division on paper while the elements were largely dispersed and already in action; contained elements of 5. and 6.FJD, training personnel, and a number of battle-groups (Kampfgruppe Menzel, Grossmehl, Laytved-Hardegg, Greve, Schaefer, Schluckebier, and Grunwald). Fought around Arnhem, and finally captured by British near Oldenburg.

8.FJD Formed in early 1945 around FJR 22 and 24; fought in Ems-Weser area until collapse in April 1945.

9.FJD Formed December 1944 from disparate elements of Luftwaffe personnel, with regiments designated FJR 25, 26 and 27. Fought on Eastern Front around Stargard, Breslau, and on the Oder; destroyed in final Russian drive on Berlin. (It was commanded by the energetic Bruno Bräuer. After resisting to the last this gallant officer was tried as a war criminal, condemned, and executed in 1947, principally for reprisals taken against Cretan partisans in 1941.)

10.FJD Drafts from 1. and 4.FJD were pulled out of Italy in March 1945 and formed into FJR 28, 29 and 30 in the Krems-Melk area of Austria. After fighting in Moravia the division largely went into Russian captivity.

11.FJD A 'paper' formation which probably never managed to bring together the dispersed elements allocated to it.

Equipment

Weapons

The Fallschirmjäger used all the standard issue Wehrmacht small arms, machine guns, mortars, rocket projectors, flamethrowers and—in the formations committed to infantry operations in 1942-45—field and medium artillery, self-propelled guns, anti-aircraft and anti-tank guns. For reasons of space the notes which follow are limited to those weapons not generally found among other types of troops.

Alongside the standard Mauser Kar 98K rifle, limited numbers of shortened, folding or 'break down' variants were issued to Fallschirmjäger. These included the Kar 98/42 and Brünn Gew 33/40, both of 7.92mm calibre with five-round fixed magazines. Apart from the folding-stock Gew 33/40 there was another, shortened version for airborne and mountain use. The Sauer 7.65mm Modell 38(H) Pistol, an automatic with an eight-round magazine, was popular in the Luftwaffe. The most noteworthy 'special' paratroop weapon was the Rheinmetall-designed 7.92mm Fallschirmjägergewehr 42 (FG42), a lightweight automatic rifle fitted with a folding bipod and bayonet, which took a 20-round detachable magazine; this had a higher muzzle velocity and rate of fire than the standard MP43/44 assault rifles, which were also issued in the second half of the war.

The special need of airborne troops for crew-served support weapons which could be air-dropped with the assault wave under multiple parachutes led to several interesting designs. The smallest was the 2.8cm schwere Panzerbüchse 41

Paratroopers man a PaK36; they wear splinter-camouflage smocks, jump trousers, but hobnailed infantry marching boots.(544/588/20A)

anti-tank gun on the lightweight Feldlafette 41 carriage. The tungsten-cored round for this 'squeeze bore' weapon was very effective for its size. Issued from 1941, the gun gradually became redundant due to tungsten shortages.

By the outbreak of war both Rheinmetall and Krupp were well advanced with studies of recoilless guns for airborne use, where weight was at a premium. The first to see combat, on Crete, was the 7.5cm LG40, originally designed by Krupp as the LG1 but modified by Rheinmetall, who gave it a new carriage. The LG40 had a useful range of 6,500m, and could be used against armour; it suffered from the usual handicap of recoilless weapons in that the back-blast made concealment impossible after the first shot. The 10.5cm LG40, 40/1 and 40/2 were scaled-up versions, varying one from another only in carriage details. Used in small numbers from 1941 onwards, they were replaced by the superior LG42. A 15cm version saw limited use from 1942. Production of recoilless weapons ceased in 1944; the abandonment of large scale airborne operations rendered them largely redundant.

Among anti-aircraft weapons the 2cm Flak38 was produced in an airborne version with a light, folding carriage which also allowed its use in the ground combat role; the 2cm MG151/20 was similarly modified. A projected 7.5cm light infantry gun designated leIG 18 F (for Fallschirmjäger) got no further than a prototype. Among infantry rocket projectors used was the 15cm Do-Gerät introduced

for airborne use in 1941, in small numbers. In 1944 a special one-shot, disposable flamethrower—the Einstossflammenwerfer 46—was added to the Fallschirmjäger arsenal; it fired a half-second burst out to about 27 metres.

Parachutes

Responsibility for parachute design in the pre-war years, originally headed by Professors Hoff and Madelung, belonged to the German Air Ministry's Technical Equipment Division; work was done at four experimental stations at Berlin, Rechlin, Darmstadt and Stuttgart. Testing with theodolite cameras led to the selection of the most desirable characteristics, and the initial Rückenpackung Zwangauslösung 1 (RZ1) was produced. Early in 1940 an improved RZ16 model was introduced, as a result of reports of excessive oscillation, and several fatal malfunctions of static line deployment. This was quickly followed into service in 1941 by the RZ20, which was standard for the rest of the war.

The canopy was 28 feet in diameter, circular, and sewn from 28 gores of white silk—by Operation *Merkur* canopies in subdued camouflage colours were also in use. It was packed in a cloth bag; a thin cord attached the apex of the folded canopy itself to the mouth of the bag, and the bag was firmly attached to the static line—a length of stout rope with a snap-hook at the end. The bagged canopy and the carefully coiled-down shroud (or rigging) lines were packed into a stout 'envelope' of fabric which clipped to the rear of the shoulder harness; from its corners two lengths of rope protruded and attached to D-rings at the hips of the harness, and the static line was carefully folded and stowed, partly under the flaps of the 'envelope'.

The stick of paratroopers rode to the target in the vulnerable but reliable Junkers Ju52/3m trimotor transport, which could accommodate between 12 and 18 men according to internal arrangement, sitting in seats down the sides of the fuselage. As they approached the DZ the despatcher—Absetzer—ordered them to their feet, and they organised themselves in line, each man holding the snap-hook end of his static line in his teeth to leave his hands free. On the order they would 'hook up'—attach the snap-hook to a stout cable anchored high along the wall of the fuselage, along which the hook could

The 10.5cm. LG40 recoilless gun manned by a Fallschirmjäger crew wearing plain grey-green smocks—and note service dress rank chevrons worn on the smock sleeve by the Obergefreiter.(546/668/7)

run as the men filed to the door. As each man reached the door he braced himself, feet spread and hands clutching rails at the edges of the door, and then launched himself outwards in a headlong dive—a tricky manoeuvre which was carefully taught during training. The static line paid out as he fell, and when its nine-metre length was fully deployed the man's weight and the forwards momentum of the aircraft to which he was still attached came to bear upon the pack. The static line pulled the flaps of the envelope apart and pulled out the bagged canopy. As the man continued to fall the bag was jerked off the canopy, and the thin link attaching bag to canopy broke. The static line and bag remained flapping outside the aircraft door; the free paratrooper continued to fall, his canopy now exposed to the airflow and developing fast, the shroud lines uncoiling between it and the body harness as the man continued to fall while the canopy 'stopped' to open. When he reached the extent of the shroud lines, he too stopped—with a violent shock.

This 'canopy first' method contrasted with the opening sequence of the British X-type parachute, in which the canopy was stowed in a tubular bag, with the rigging lines separately folded down to the the back pack (or bag) in an even zig-zag, each bunch held by elastic bands. As the British pack opened the bag was pulled out in a long 'sausage', and the balance of forces bearing on it was such that the rigging lines whipped out of their bands in an orderly sequence and deployed to their full extent *before* the bag was jerked off the canopy, allowing it to open. This lengthened the whole opening sequence considerably, giving the paratrooper a relatively more gradual deceleration and a much less violent opening shock. But the German method had the advantage of allowing jumps from lower altitudes, a valuable consideration for a man who may be a sitting target for ground fire while he hangs helpless beneath his canopy. Altitudes of 380 to 400 feet were normal, and one of the lifts in the Crete invasion jumped safely from 250 feet. The canopy was reckoned to be fully deployed by the

23

Paratrooper firing the FG42 from its bipod; he wears the Zeltbahn shelter-half as a rainproof over his smock. (738/289/16)

time the Fallschirmjäger had fallen about 120 feet.

The great disadvantage of the RZ series rigs lay in the harness attachment, and is inexplicable, considering the generally excellent standard of all German military equipment. The harness itself was fairly conventional, a variant of the classic Irvin design with crossways waist, chest, and thigh straps united by vertical webs up each side of the chest and crossing behind the back: see plates A1, A2, D1 and F2. But where the Allied parachutes had vertical 'lift webs' rising in front and behind the shoulders to unite to the bottoms of the two groups of shroud lines, the RZ followed the old Italian Salvatore design in having the shrouds uniting at a single point behind and above the shoulders; the canopy and shrouds attached to the harness only by a V-shaped rope strop joining this single point to D-rings behind the hips of the waist web.

The consequences of this were several, and all bad. Firstly, the Fallschirmjäger's famous headlong dive from the door was a necessary precaution rather than bravado: he *had* to be horizontal when the 'chute opened, even though the shock must have doubled him up painfully, jerking head and feet towards one another. If he had been falling in the conventional upright position when the RZ's violent opening shock hit him so low down on his body, he would have flipped upside down, with a good chance of tangling his feet in the shroud lines as they whipped out above him—an accident which could prove fatal.

Secondly, during his descent he was unable to reach up and grab the shroud lines or webs attached to them. It is by pulling on one or other of the four 'lift webs' that paratroopers with conventional rigs spill air selectively from one or other part of the canopy lip; and this is how they steer themselves relative to the target—e.g. spilling at the back of the canopy gives some forward speed. It is also how they face into the wind when about to land—pulling down hard on one web rotates the paratrooper in that direction, with quite exact control. Facing into the wind opposes the parachute's slight natural forward speed to that of the wind, achieving the slowest possible drift across the DZ at the moment of landing. The Fallschirmjäger was thus a plaything of the wind, unable to control where he fell, how fast, or in what direction.

The lack of control over cross-ground speed became poignant at the moment of landing; for the low attachment forced the Fallschirmjäger to fall in a 'leaning forwards' posture. At the last moment he might succeed in facing round into the direction in which he seemed to be drifting, by means of vague swimming motions of the arms and legs, and then he inevitably faced a 'forward roll' landing. This explains the importance given by the Fallschirmjäger to padded protection for knees, ankles and wrists—almost unknown among Allied paratroopers. Readers should not be misled by memories of seeing modern sports parachutists making effortless 'stand-up' landings under today's sophisticated parafoil canopies. A forward roll landing by a heavily-laden man under a World War II military parachute, descending at a rate of between 12 and 19 feet per second even under calm wind conditions, was a thoroughly dangerous undertaking; fractures on the DZ were quite common.

Whether or not he got down in one piece, the Fallschirmjäger's inability to get free of his harness quickly (he had four buckles to undo, instead of the British paratrooper's single quick-release box), and his inability to reach up and pull selected shroud lines at once and from any position, exposed him to a final danger. In high or gusting wind there is a serious possibility of being dragged across the DZ by a canopy which refuses to collapse—dragged into water, perhaps, or literally dragged to death on rough ground. The German paratrooper's greater difficulty in pulling in the shrouds attached to the

1: Obergefreiter, II/FJR 1; Brunswick, Germany, 1939
2: Jäger, Fallschirmjäger-Regiment 1, 1941
3: Unteroffizier, FJR 1; Stendal, Germany, 1939

A

1: Oberleutnant, I/FJR 1; Western Europe, spring 1940
2,3: Jäger, and NCO, Low Countries, May 1940

1

3

2

B

C

1,2: Jäger, 7.Flieger-Div.; Operation 'Merkur', May 1941
3: Major, III/FJR 1; Crete, May 1941

1: Hauptmann, Fallschirmjäger-Bde. Ramcke; N.Africa, 1942
2: Feldwebel, Fallschirmjäger-Bde. Ramcke; N.Africa, 1942
3: Jäger, I/FJR 5; Tunisia, spring 1943

E

1: General der Flieger Kurt Student, 1944
2: Major, 1.Fallschirmjäger-Div.; Berlin, 1944
3: Jäger, Italy, 1944

F

1: Oberleutnant, Russia, 1942-43
2: Ski trooper, 1.FJD; Russia, 1943
3: Jäger, 5.FJD; Ardennes, December 1944

G

1: Jäger, 2.FJD; France, 1944
2: Oberfeldwebel, StuG-Bde.XII; Reichswald, January 1945
3: Unteroffizier, 9.FJD; Eastern Front, spring 1945

H

owest part of the canopy lip to collapse it increased his danger of being dragged.

The horrors of the RZ rig are the harder to understand when one recalls that Luftwaffe aircrew had a parachute harness with conventional Irvin-style shoulder webs. We know that in mid-1943 the Germans developed a triangular parachute with better control characteristics, but this RZ36 apparently never saw service.

Fallschirmjäger jump training was thorough, preparing men to overcome the drawbacks of their equipment as well as possible. Basic landing techniques were learned under gymnasium conditions. Familiarity with and correct handling of the parachute itself was taught at an early stage, quickly followed by an introduction to packing technique. This continued while the volunteer progressed to simulated jumps from a dummy fuselage, and sessions in a captive harness. By the time air training commenced he had mastered the fairly simple but vital skill of packing, and thereafter only jumped rigs he had packed himself. Six training jumps were made, the first alone and from about 600 feet, the others in groups, under varying light conditions, and from progressively lower altitudes. The final jump was made by 36 men from three aircraft, from less than 400 feet, and was immediately followed by a tactical exercise on the ground. Successful qualification brought the coveted *Fallschirmschützenabzeichen*.

Containers

Unlike his Allied counterparts, who could jump with fairly massive equipment bags attached to their harness and released to dangle on a rope before they landed, the Fallschirmjäger could carry only the lightest personal kit and weapons. He was reliant on separate air-dropped containers—Waffenhälter—for main weapons, ammunition, food, medical supplies, communications equipment, and everything else he would need before the arrival of air-landing troops and transports. Since containers often fell some way from the inevitably more or less scattered men, recovery could be a life-

Interesting Fallschirmjäger group photographed in 1944. Left centre, note special gasmask bag slung on the chest; at right is the butt of an FG42; and two men wear the Einheitsfeldmütze 1943 which replaced the sidecap.(582/2105/16)

and-death affair—on Crete this scramble to reach containers under the guns of the defenders cost many lives.

At the time of Operation *Merkur* there were at least three different sizes of container in use; smaller types would be used for heavy loads such as ammunition, and larger ones for light but bulky loads such as medical supplies. After Crete (and thus rather late in the day to be of practical use) the Luftwaffe standardised on a container of square section, five feet long and 16 inches on a side, with rounded edges and several handles. A small pair of rubber-tyred wheels and a T-shaped pulling handle were stowed inside so that the container could be used as a cart to drag equipment off the DZ. The loaded weight was 260lb., and 14 were needed for the equipment of a full-strength platoon of 43 men. A crushable corrugated metal base-pad at the lower end acted as a shock-absorber, and a parachute was packed at the other end. Containers were normally carried on special racks inside the cargo bays of the Ju52s, but could also be carried externally under the wings of the Junkers or of other aircraft such as the He111. (See Plate D.)

The Plates

A1: Obergefreiter, II/FJR 1; Brunswick, Germany, 1939
This former member of the Army's Fallschirm-Infanterie-Bataillon retains the green jump smock first adopted by that unit; this was seen for some time after the battalion was incorporated into the Luftwaffe. Collarless, it had two zips from throat to thigh, with press-fastened tabs high on the chest to prevent the zips from becoming unfastened. It was notably shorter than later patterns, and had a gathered effect at the hem. The Army's straight-winged national emblem was worn on the right breast (and may be seen on Luftwaffe smocks, in isolated cases, well into 1940); and conventional Army rank chevrons are worn on the left sleeve. The special paratrooper's trousers, in a greenish field grey, were shaped similarly to the general issue 1943 Wehrmacht field trousers. They were gathered at

The classic model of Fallschirmjäger helmet cover is worn by this MG42 gunner; note broad foliage band, crossed strips over the crown, and spring-hook attachments. He has acquired a US Army 'pineapple' as well as his Wehrmacht-izsue 'egg' grenades.(579/1957/26A)

the ankle by tapes and buttons, and had two side and two hip pockets, plus a small 'fob' pocket on the front of the right hip. In the side seam outside the knee on each side were slits, closed by press fasteners, allowing the removal of the rectangular kapok-filled canvas knee pads which were tied directly over the kneecaps with tapes. The left leg slit is usually invisible in photos; the right leg slit had a special pocket sewn immediately behind it, fastened by three large press-studs, for the gravity knife. (This was a large jack-knife with a blade which slid into or out of the handle by its own weight and the one-handed operation of a locking catch, for use in emergencies to cut free tangled shroud lines.)

In addition to the internal pads, external tubular knee pads were worn for the jump. Of leather-covered sponge rubber, they were fastened by crossed, elasticated straps. The early pattern jump boots were distinguished by lacing up the outside of the instep and ankle rather than the front; they had heavy rubber soles with a chevron pattern. The definitive paratrooper's helmet is worn by figure *A2*; painted Luftwaffe blue-grey, it bears two

Gen. Kurt Student inspecting paratroopers somewhere in the Mediterranean theatre; they wear 'second pattern Luftwaffe' jump smocks in splinter camouflage, and sandy-drill tropical trousers. For details of Student's uniform and decorations, see Plate F1.(569/1589/8)

decals: the national tricolour shield on the right, and a reversed form of the white Luftwaffe eagle on the left. Note *A1's* slit-brim early-model helmet. For the jump paratroopers wore black leather gauntlets with elasticated cuffs.

The parachute harness appeared in two slightly different forms; this is the type seen in pre-war photos, and may have been associated with the early RZ1 parachute. (The RZ16 pack appeared in 1940, and the RZ20 in 1941; association of the early harness with the RZ1, and the later type worn by figure *A2* with the RZ16 or RZ20, is speculative.) The early harness had two simple shoulder webs which crossed between the shoulder blades (see under figure *F2*), with D-rings for attaching the pack just above the crossing point. The pack seen in early photos is distinguished by vertical stowage of the folded lengths of static line on the right side of the rear face of the pack, with the white stores label displayed vertically on the left side surface or left

Inside Cassino, 1944. The two men at the left wear Army windproof anoraks in field grey—note pullover construction and chest pocket. Three helmet styles are represented here: plain blue-grey, overpainted sandy yellow, and with the splinter camouflage cover.(578/1926/34)

the so-called 'first pattern Luftwaffe' smock, used by the Air Force parachute unit from its inception. Of the same kind of greenish cotton drill material as the Army type, it had a fall collar; two short, permanently tailored-in 'legs' into which the wearer had to step when putting it on; and a single, central front join—initially buttoned, later zipped—covered by a fly and extending from throat to crotch. Early versions had no front pockets, but slit side pockets. The Luftwaffe national emblem was worn on the right breast in white thread on blue backing. A white-on-green version specifically for use on the smock was later produced. This smock is also reported to have been made in grey material.

A3: Unteroffizier, FJR 1; Stendal, Germany, 1939
This NCO wears standard Luftwaffe service dress for junior NCOs ('NCOs without Portepee') of all branches, with Parachute Troops distinctions. The *Schirmmütze* or service cap is Luftwaffe blue with a black ribbed band, black patent peak and strap, pressed alloy insignia of conventional Luftwaffe design, and piping in branch-of-service colour at crown seam and band edges—here, the golden yellow of aircrew and parachute troops. The fly-fronted *Fliegerbluse* was worn open-necked and without a shirt and tie for service dress, and open over a pale blue shirt and black tie for walking out. Initially it had no pockets for NCOs and men; from November 1940 side pockets were introduced, slanted, with buttoned, round-cornered flaps. (Officers' blouses had flapless 'slash' side pockets.) The collar bears patches in branch colour, with alloy 'eagles' indicating rank: from one to four, identifying the junior ranks from Jäger to Hauptgefreiter; and from one to four, accompanied by the usual German NCOs' silver braid or *Tresse* around the upper collar, for ranks from Unteroffizier to Stabsfeldwebel. All enlisted ranks wore piping in branch colour—*Waffenfarbe*—round the outer edge of the upper collar. Shoulder straps for all enlisted ranks had outer piping in *Waffenfarbe*; from this rank upwards, *Tresse* and silver-grey pips in various combinations identified exact ranks. Below Unteroffizier, silver-grey left sleeve chevrons identified the ranks of Gefreiter (one), Obergefreiter (two), and Hauptgefreiter (three); two chevrons with a pip in the 'bite' identified the rank of Stabsgefreiter from February 1944 onwards. The blouse is worn

edge of the rear face, and the doubled sections of line forming the attachment strap to the harness hip D-rings passing under the pack flaps at the lower corners. The later harness, worn here by *A2*, had a cloth shoulder yoke incorporating the shoulder webs; the static line seems generally to have been stowed horizontally on the top of the rear face, and the attachments from the hip D-rings passed upwards to disappear under the flaps at the upper corners of the pack. We know that early issue parachutes suffered repeated failures of static line deployment, and may guess that the visible changes to the arrangement of the pack were safety improvements.

A2: Jäger, Fallschirmjäger-Regiment 1, 1941
Points of difference are the modifications to the pack and harness discussed above; and the smock. This is

with straight Luftwaffe blue-grey trousers and standard Wehrmacht marching boots. The belt has a Luftwaffe buckle; Air Force leatherwork was initially dark brown.

The Luftwaffe's 'wavy winged' national emblem was worn on the right breast as standard only from March 1940, and was often absent from the blouse before then. On the left is the Luftwaffe Para-chutist's Badge, instituted in November 1936, with a silver-finish oak and laurel wreath (blackened, from late 1942) and a gold eagle. (The Army equivalent, instituted in June 1937, was retained instead by ex-members of the Army parachute unit who qualified between that date and January 1939. It had a gold wreath entirely of oakleaves, with the folded-wing Wehr-macht eagle and swastika at the top centre, and the diving eagle, in silver, had empty talons.) This *Fallschirmschützenabzeichen* was awarded on com-pletion of training and six jumps, and—officially—the wearer had to re-qualify each year to retain it.

The cuff title on the right forearm bears the silver-grey lettering *Fallschirm-Jäger Rgt. 1* on green cloth; the officers' version had silver lettering and silver edges. An identical though suitably numbered band was worn by members of FJR 2; and personnel of other elements of 7.Flieger-Division and the Stendal parachute school wore a similar one lettered *Fallschirm-Division*—though this did not have edging on the officers' version. Note that all three were ordered discontinued shortly after the outbreak of war in 1939, and photos of them being worn are rare.

B1: Oberleutnant, I/FJR 1; Western Europe, spring 1940
This officer on the DZ is removing his jump smock in order to get at his personal equipment; this was worn beneath the smock for the jump, then put on over it after landing. (This unwieldy procedure, made the more time-consuming by the lack of a quick-release buckle on the 'chute harness and by the 'step-in' design of the first pattern smock, was felt to be necessary because of the danger of equipment worn exposed becoming tangled in the shroud lines at the moment of opening.) He wears the usual paratrooper's helmet; photos in fact show that the units which jumped over Norway in 1940 contained a fair number of men wearing con-ventional general issue steel helmets, and some with

the early experimental model cut down from the general issue helmet, most easily identified in photos by a small horizontal slit in the brim ahead of the ear. The 'first pattern' smock was acquiring pockets during 1940; the three figures on this plate show some variations. Many had a single slanted pocket on the left breast; others, the breast pocket and two horizontally-fastened front thigh pockets. These early examples seem always to have the white plastic zip exposed, i.e. not covered by a fly flap as was normal by 1941. Stylised rank patches were also beginning to be worn, the same as those made for the Luftwaffe aircrew flying suits. White cloth shapes on tan or dark blue backing identified exact rank: for officers, one to three 'eagles' over one bar for Leutnant, Oberleutnant and Hauptmann; one to three 'eagles' over two bars for Major, Oberstleutnant and Oberst.

Beneath his smock he wears the officers' version of the *Fliegerbluse*, with silver twist piping around the upper collar in place of the yellow of enlisted ranks. His collar patches, in yellow *Waffenfarbe*, are also edged with silver twist. They bear ranking much as the sequence described above, with one, two and three 'eagles' over an oakleaf spray for subalterns, and one, two and three wholly enclosed by a wreath for field officers; all insignia on officers' patches was embroidered. The right breast national emblem is

This paratrooper in Italy displays the front pocket detail of the jump trousers; note makeshift camouflage helmet cover made from Italian Army material.(579/1953/20)

Interesting group which includes Fallschirmjäger and what appear to be Italian paratroopers (right). Whether these men are still in Italian service, or are men of the 'Folgore' or 'Nembo' Divisions re-assigned to 4.FJD upon its formation in winter 1943/44 is not clear. The German at the left wears an infantry helmet and an old grey-green smock; the man next to him wears an Italian paratroop helmet and a German splinter smock.(578/1931/7A)

also in silver embroidery. Junior officers' shoulder straps were in silver 'Russia braid' on a *Waffenfarbe* backing, plain for Leutnant, and with one and two gold pips for Oberleutnant and Hauptmann.

Personal equipment worn on the jump was minimal. This officer would wear the usual brown Wehrmacht officer's field belt with a two-claw steel frame buckle, a holstered Luger P08 on the left hip, a mapcase, a water canteen, a gasmask in the special paratroops' field grey cloth container slung round his neck, and probably nothing else.

B2 and B3: Jäger and NCO, Low Countries, May 1940
These two soldiers wear essentially the same clothing and equipment. *B2*, a man of FJR 1 fighting in Holland, has the tricolour shield painted over on his helmet, for camouflage, but retains the eagle decal. He has reached the supply canisters,

and carries the standard Wehrmacht Mauser Kar 98K rifle, and two boxes of machine gun belts for the section MG34. He wears his field equipment over his smock: belt, Y-straps, the holstered automatic pistol carried by all personnel on the jump, gasmask bag, 'breadbag' and canteen behind the right hip, and perhaps an entrenching spade and bayonet behind the left. The most interesting item, which was in use by 1940, was the bandolier for 100 rounds of rifle ammunition, made in blue-grey material with press-fastened pockets (note upper pair on each side have only one opening edge). This was worn on the drop under the smock. It had loops for the belt on the rear surface, to prevent flapping.

The NCO, figure *B3*, does not wear sleeve rank patches—these seem to have been rare in 1940. He represents a man of Major Witzig's assault group at Eben Emael, and is taken from two of the very few confirmed photos of that unit. The helmets all seem to have been heavily smeared with mud for camouflage. The smocks seem mostly to have a single left breast pocket. The photographed groups seem to have one MP38/40 sub-machine gun to about every fourth man; they appear to wear a single set of triple magazine pouches, and all retain the holstered pistol. His smock is one of the type with thigh pockets, which are full of 'egg-grenades'. Note the Wehrmacht issue torch buttoned to the front of the partly opened smock—a typical item for a junior leader. The question of how the MP40 was carried on the jump is discussed under figures C1 and C2; but in this particular case it does not arise, since the Eben Emael assault party landed by glider.

C1: Jäger, III/ or IV/Luftlande-Sturm-Regiment (?); Operation 'Merkur', 20 May 1941
(Unit identification is highly tentative, and simply by comparison with other photos in what seems to be the same sequence of snapshots.) By the Crete operation the first helmet covers were being observed; a common type was made from the same type of greenish cloth as the smock, and had an added hessian band attached round the skull in a series of loops for foliage. The cover fixed to the helmet brim with six spring hooks. (This plain green cover was retained in many cases until very late in the war.) The smock is still of the 'first pattern' step-in type, but now has four pockets, all with zips covered by 'letter box' flaps. This paratrooper, just about to emplane, holds the static line in his teeth in the regulation manner, to leave his hands free.

The most interesting points are his weapon and ammunition. Unusually, he has tied the magazine pouches to his shins below the knee pads. What is clearly an MP40 with stock folded is carried jammed under his harness in what seems to be a cover made from paratrooper's gasmask bags. This position, between his body and the waist web to which the shroud lines and V-strop were attached by D-rings at the hip, appears to ensure that the opening shock of the parachute will be transmitted directly to the gun, smashing it against his ribcage with crushing force . . . one cannot imagine how the inspecting NCO let the fool past him!

C2: Feldwebel, 7.Flieger-Division; Operation 'Merkur', 20 May 1941
The Crete assault saw the introduction of numbers of the so-called 'second pattern' jump smock. This was superficially very similar to the first type, but

was made in green splinter-pattern camouflage material. More significantly, the 'step-in' design was abandoned; it made removal of the smock to reach the equipment—or to relieve oneself!—a lengthy business. The second pattern had an opening from throat to hem, and a system of press-studs around the edge of the 'skirt' which allowed it to be buttoned into 'legs' for the jump, and, if wished, left loose thereafter. Crete also saw the first use of some examples of a helmet cover in the same splinter camouflage material; the characteristic construction was in four main panels, with a separate crown-piece showing a cross of material, a band of foliage loops around the skull, and the same hooked edge as the plain green cover. The next four years saw many minor variations of this cover; some had very narrow bands of loops, some were sewn together in different ways, and some were fixed by a simple drawstring under the rim of the helmet.

Sleeve rank patches seem to have been widespread by May 1941, and for NCOs bore from one to four 'eagles', and four 'eagles' with a 'pip' below, for

Italian paratrooper in Italian helmet and distinctive camouflage smock, photographed serving either in 4.FJD or alongside a German paratroop unit.(578/1931/11A)

Fallschirmjäger in Russia wearing reversible, quilted winter combat clothing with the white side outwards.(578/1940/2)

the ranks of Unteroffizier, Unterfeldwebel, Feld-webel, Oberfeldwebel, and Stabsfeldwebel. The side-lacing jump boots now began to be replaced by a front-laced version, simpler to manufacture and perfectly efficient: the practical value of the side-laced type is hard to imagine. The harness of the parachute is slightly modified, with buckles of patent design replacing the earlier D-rings and spring slips at some points, and replacing the simpler buckle on the waist web. The original photo is one of several showing men preparing for the Crete drop with the old kapok-filled Luftwaffe life-jacket worn back to front over their harness, its open 'front' loosely thonged in place around the pack. The Crete operation obviously involved a real danger of coming down in the sea; but common sense suggests that this lifejacket may have been discarded before jumping, and was intended for use only if the transport 'ditched' with its stick still on board. Its practical value as a life preserver when worn in this manner seems minimal; and to jump with it tied on firmly enough to resist the airstream would greatly increase the chances of a parachute malfunction, since the tapes could so easily foul the static line or pack flaps.

Note also the MP40 loosely attached to the harness to hang by the left thigh—more practical than the method attempted by figure $C1$, but still potentially dangerous on landing, given the forward roll landing technique. There does not seem to be any evidence of officially approved methods of carrying the MP40 on the jump; yet several sources state that the dangers of landing armed only with a pistol, perhaps far from the containers of heavier weapons, were well known by 1941; and that about one man in four carried MP40s for the Crete drop and *all* personnel for subsequent drops. It is worth adding that photos taken at the Stendal school definitely show men falling with rifles held in their hands; but how this was accomplished, and whether it was an operational practice, remain a mystery.

C3: Leutnant, 7.Flieger-Division; Operation 'Merkur', May 1941

Wearing the four-pocket *Tuchrock* instead of the *Fliegerbluse* with the field uniform was an affectation one notices in photos of several officers—e.g. Oberst Brauer of FJR 1, and Hauptmann Schirmer of II/FJR 2 at Heraklion. The peaked *Schirmmütze* was obviously not carried on the jump—though some officers seem to have recovered theirs surprisingly soon after landing—and the usual field headgear was the 'little ship', the *Fliegermütze* sidecap worn by figure *D3*. This officer has only to put on his smock and parachute, and exchange cap for helmet, and he is ready to emplane.

The peaked service cap was identical for officers of all Luftwaffe branches; all had silver wire insignia, silver piping at crown seam and band edges, and silver cords. The four-pocket service tunic bore essentially the same insignia as the field blouse: shoulder straps of rank and branch, silver wire Luftwaffe eagle, silver collar piping, and the same silver-wire-and-*Waffenfarbe* collar patches of rank. A woven version of the *Fallschirm-*

schützabzeichen was available for field use; officers' versions were in silver and gold wire, enlisted ranks' in white and yellow thread. The grades of the Iron Cross were awarded in order; the 2nd Class was not displayed, its ribbon normally being worn in the tunic buttonhole, while the subsequent 1st Class award was pin-backed and always displayed on the left pocket.

D1: Jäger, 7.Flieger-Division. Operation 'Merkur', May 1941

This illustrates the awkward landing position described in the body of the text.

D2: Jäger. 7.Flieger-Division, Operation 'Merkur', May 1941

Photos show that the Crete assault units still wore many bare helmets alongside those covered with green or camouflage cloth. The smock was often worn directly over the bare torso in the Mediterranean heat, with sleeves rolled; this is the

A paratrooper in action with the Flammenwerfer 41 on the Russian Front.(553/841/4)

Peaceful domestic scene taken in France, 1944: men of a Fallschirmjäger light flak battery with a 'prisoner'. (582/2116/29)

camouflaged 'second pattern' smock, with flies covering the white plastic zips of the four pockets. Light belt equipment is worn—photos of the early fighting on Crete seldom show more than belt, Y-straps, canteen, breadbag, and ammunition. This is one of the lucky paratroopers who lived to reach the weapons containers on the fire-swept DZ.

We show here the container standardised after the Crete operation, although similar items of several sizes were used for that assault. Bright colours and identifying bands and symbols were used to speed up the frantic process of recovery: a radio equipment container was photographed with a large signals 'blitz' sign marked in some mid-tone colour along the apparently white-painted sides, and a medical container had red crosses on white discs painted on all sides. The paratrooper is retrieving a Mauser rifle from this standard weapons-and-ammunition container.

D3: Major, III/FJR 1; Crete, May 1941
Normal field headgear for all ranks was the *Fliegermütze* or '*Schiffchen*', a blue-grey sidecap which differed from the Army model in having a smoothly tapered upper line to the turn-up band, rather than the 'scallop' shape which theoretically allowed the turn-up to be lowered for ear protection. Officers and men wore caps identical apart from quality, and a line of silver piping round the officers' turn-up. The national eagle in white (silver for officers) was sewn to the crown, and a raised boss presentation of the national cockade to the band. The cap was gradually replaced from late 1943 by the *Einheitsfeldmütze* worn by figure *H3*. (On Crete, where tropical uniform items became available in small numbers only, and later in Sicily and Italy, where paratroopers retreating from Africa and others coming from Europe fought together, official regulations forbidding the mixing of tropical and European uniform items were widely ignored.)

The Luftwaffe's tropical uniform is to be seen in only a few photographs of the invasion of Crete; this figure is taken from one of Maj. Karl-Lothar Schulz, commander of 3rd Bn., Fallschirmjäger-Regiment 1. The tunic is of a strong yellowish shade of cotton drill, quite different from the faded olive green of the Army, and of a different cut. It lacks the collar piping of European uniforms; and collar patches were not normally attached. Schulz wore them, however, and another photo shows them on the tropical tunic of Obstlt. Heilmann of FJR 3 in Sicily. The usual shoulder straps of rank and branch were worn on the tropical tunic; for field officers these were of interwoven braid, on *Waffenfarbe* underlay, and Oberstleutnant and Oberst were identified by one and two gold 'pips'. The tunic was made with the national breast emblem already sewn in place, in the blue-grey or white thread on a tan backing worn by enlisted ranks; few officers seem to have bothered to replace this with their silver-on-blue insignia.

E1: Hauptmann, Fallschirmjäger-Brigade Ramcke; North Africa, August 1942

The tropical tunic worn with its matching trousers, distinguished by the large left thigh pocket, and by the loose shape, gathered at the ankle and here worn over rather than tucked into the jump boots. When smartness was required a khaki drill shirt with a matching or brown tie were worn: in the field the shirt was worn open or with a scarf. The summer version of the normal Luftwaffe officer's *Schirmmütze*, with the unpiped crown in a loosely woven white cloth, was popular in Africa; alternatives for officers were the 'Meyer' (see *E2*), or a silver-piped officer's version of the tropical sidecap (see *E3*).

Two insignia are noteworthy. On the right breast is the Spanish Cross in Silver with Swords, the third of six classes of this decoration, awarded to mark courage or meritorious service with the Condor Legion in Spain, 1936 to 1939. Several parachute personnel were photographed wearing this decoration; a small experimental group may have served in Spain, but details are obscure, and the decoration could have been earned while serving in some other branch of the Legion. Sewn on the right forearm is the Luftwaffe's *Afrika* cuff title; in silver on dark blue for officers and with light grey lettering for enlisted ranks, this was awarded between February 1942 and February 1943 to all Luftwaffe personnel serving in Africa. In the latter month it was replaced by the all-service pattern cuff title worn on the left forearm—the familiar grey-on-brown '*Afrika*-with-palms' design.

E2: Feldwebel, Fallschirmjäger-Brigade Ramcke; North Africa, autumn 1942

The Luftwaffe's special tropical field cap, called a 'Meyer' cap in a rather elaborately joking reference to Göring which is not funny enough to justify the space for an explanation, was worn to some extent by both officers and enlisted ranks of parachute units and the 'Hermann Göring' Division in the Mediterranean from April 1942 onwards. It was an alternative to the more common peaked tropical field cap worn by figure *F3*. Of sandy drill cloth with a scarlet lining, it had flat-woven white insignia of conventional Luftwaffe design, a light leather chinstrap, and an optional button-on neck flap. Officers sometimes substituted cap cords, of either silver or matt white cord.

The Luftwaffe tropical shirt differed from the Army pattern in buttoning right down the front. It was seen both with and without the right breast eagle, which was embroidered on a triangular tan backing. Otherwise the only insignia attached to it—apart from metal awards pinned on for parades—were the shoulder straps. Both the European uniform blue-grey straps and a special tropical version were observed; the latter, shown here, had a sandy drill ground, with normal *Waffenfarbe* piping but *Tresse*, if any, in a dull brown.

Generalleutnant Ramcke, commanding 2.FJD, photographed with paratroop and Panzer officers in 1944. His division was largely wiped off the order of battle in the siege of Brest. It is unusual to see colar patches worn on a greatcoat. (580/1988/16A)

Fine study of a paratroop section in Normandy, 1944. At left, note soldier with captured Bren gun; two men wear infantry helmets; all seem to wear the early grey-green jump smock, and note Luftwaffe eagle decal still on helmets at this late date.(576/1846/19a)

The shorts issued as part of the tropical outfit were long and full, and photos often show them turned up for smartness. This NCO wears them with the usual Luftwaffe belt fitted with a full set of the tropical issue all-canvas MP38/40 magazine pouches (note small tool pouch on left set only); his blue-grey socks are turned down over jump boots, which now began to appear in brown leather as well as black. The Army's brown leather hobnailed ankle boots, and canvas and leather tropical boots, were also worn.

E3: Jäger, I/FJR 5; Tunisia, spring 1943
The tropical version of the Luftwaffe *Fliegermütze* was the normal headgear in this theatre. The national emblem was in pale blue-grey embroidery on a tan backing, and the usual black-white-red cockade was in raised boss form. (Photos suggest that while some officers wore a version with silver piping round the edge of the false turn-up, many wore the enlisted ranks' cap unadorned, and few

bothered to fit officers' silver insignia.) The jump smock, either of green or of splinter camouflage, was worn in Africa. There is no evidence for the existence of a tan cloth version, although a photo shown to me by an acquaintance in Australia suggests that some may have been privately ordered—the smock in question even had the cloth bandoliers integral to the fronts of the garment; but for lack of positive confirmation I have not illustrated it. Conventional bandoliers were made in tropical drill cloth, however. Another piece of combat equipment quite widely used by para-troopers was a set of canvas 'waterwing' bags for stick grenades.

Hans Teske, who served with FJR 5 after transferring from the Sturm-Regiment, recalls that in his 1.Kompanie of this battalion all personnel wore blue and white silk polka-dot scarves. He also remembers that the helmet, camouflage-painted in sand colour of a slightly pinkish shade, and sometimes with sand mixed in with the paint for a matt effect, was sometimes marked on the left side with a company emblem. This was a comet—recalling the emblem used later in the war by 4.Fallschirmjäger-Division—but in company colours. The headquarters company wore a white comet with an eau-de-nil edging; 1.Kompanie wore black edged with white.

The weapon is the 'break-down' Brünn Gew 33/40, issued in small numbers to parachute troops.

F1: General der Flieger Kurt Student, 1944

The 'Father of the Fallschirmtruppe' wears regulation Luftwaffe general officer's service dress. The service dress cap is exactly like that worn by all other officer ranks, except that all insignia, piping, cords and buttons are in gold. The *Tuchrock* has gold buttons, collar piping, and national breast emblem. Collar patch and shoulder strap backing was white for general officers. The patches, edged gold, bore gold 'eagles' enclosed in a gold wreath: one, two and three for Generalmajor, Generalleutnant and General. The rank of Generaloberst was identified by similar patches with a large gold Luftwaffe eagle above crossed batons, the eagle's wings breaking the wreath. Shoulder straps bore mixed silver and gold interwoven braid, with no 'pips', and one, two and three silver 'pips' respectively, for the four general ranks. The service dress breeches bore broad white stripes with central white piping.

Student's personal awards are the Knight's Cross worn at the throat; his Pilot/Observer's Badge on the left pocket; below this the silver 'bar' marking a second World War repeat award of the Iron Cross 1st Class he won in the First World War, immediately above that medal; on the left, as viewed, the Silver Wound Badge, and on the right the large silver Pilot's Badge of the Imperial Air Service.

On his left forearm is the yellow-on-white *Kreta* cuff title awarded to commemorate that campaign to all ranks of all services who had taken part in the battle between 19 and 27 May 1941. Contrary to some accounts, Student did indeed land on Crete.

F2: Major, 1.Fallschirmjäger-Division; Berlin, May 1944

A composite figure, taken from photos of an investiture parade at which Göring decorated personnel for gallantry at Cassino, and from a photo of Maj. Freiherr von der Heydte. It was the unique practice of the German parachute troops to wear for some parades a version of the parachute harness over a clean and pressed jump smock and field uniform, complete with all decorations. Various sources describe this harness as 'simplified'; it is hard

General der Flieger Student, right, with paratroop officers, apparently during an exercise in North-West Europe (see white umpire's hatband worn by Oberleutnant in centre) during 1944.(544/585/31)

to see how it differed from the normal early-pattern harness, apart from being slackened off to achieve a smart effect, and apart from the obvious absence of the pack itself. (The small inset shows the layout of webs in the rear of the early harness.) The insignia and awards shown here are the normal national emblem on the right breast, above the War Order of the German Cross in Gold; and on the left, rather cramped to fit in the spaces between the harness webs, the Iron Cross 1st Class, the Parachutist's Badge, the Luftwaffe Ground Combat Badge, and a Wound Badge. The *Kreta* cuff title is worn on the smock; and conventional rank patches are sewn to both sleeves. In theory, some officers and men would qualify to wear both the grey and brown '*Afrika*-with-palms' title and the *Kreta* title on the smock for such parades; photos certainly exist of both being worn, *Afrika* butted immediately above *Kreta*, on the left sleeve of the service tunic.

F3: Jäger, Italy, 1944

As mentioned above, a mixture of tropical and European uniform items were often seen in Italy. The Luftwaffe version of the general issue tropical field cap was in the pale sandy shade of the Luftwaffe tropical uniform; it bore the same insignia as the sidecap, figure *E3*. The jump smock appeared in the camouflage known as 'tan water pattern' in 1943–45, and all three types—green, 'splinter' and 'water'—could be observed in simultaneous use. (In 1944–45 there was also some use of smocks made up from stocks of Italian Army camouflage material.) Since the great majority of paratroopers fought as infantry after 1941, there was an increasing use of items of conventional infantry equipment and uniform. This man wears general issue hobnail ankle boots, a general issue gasmask canister, and black Army Y-straps.

The dull yellowish webbing assault frame clipped to the rear of the Y-straps and belt supports a messtin and a splinter-camouflage poncho; below this is a bag for bivouac equipment. From the belt are slung the breadbag and canteen, a folding entrenching spade, and a bayonet; despite the erosion of the airborne rôle the holstered Luger or Walther seems generally to have been retained on the left hip. The weapon is the FG42; note also the special bandolier for its magazines, which was made in blue, tan or splinter-camouflage cloth, with eight pockets each closed by two press-studs on the 'inner' edge as worn. Helmets in Italy and North-West Europe were often covered with string foliage netting of the appropriate colour, in the absence of cloth helmet covers.

G1: Oberleutnant, Russia, 1942–43
Parachute troops fighting as infantry on the Eastern Front received the full range of Army single-sided or reversible protective clothing in addition to their own special field dress. The photo from which we take this figure shows the trousers of the padded, reversible mouse-grey/white winter suit, worn over the green jump smock; the latter has rank patches on blue backing, from a Luftwaffe winter flying suit. The helmet, field equipment, and even the gauntlets and binoculars have been roughly whitewashed for camouflage effect.

G2: Ski trooper, 1.Fallschirmjäger-Division; Russia, 1943
As well as the whitewashed helmet, and the normal blue uniform headgear, photos show some issue of this special Luftwaffe winter version of the 1943 *Einheitsfeldmütze*, in natural sheepskin with added peak and insignia. The snow camouflage outfit is loose and thin, being worn over protective clothing purely for concealment; the coloured cloth bands buttoned to the upper arms were generally used throughout the Wehrmacht as temporary 'field signs', to distinguish troops from Russian soldiers in similar snow suits.

G3: Jäger, 5.Fallschirmjäger-Division; Ardennes, December 1944
By this stage of the war a great deal of general issue material could be seen worn by paratroopers, many of whom had probably never jumped in their lives. The special helmet was increasingly painted in Army greyish-green; chicken-wire was a common expedient for the attachment of foliage. The helmet is worn here over a wool toque. The conventional blue-grey Luftwaffe greatcoat is worn for warmth, and over it an item quite frequently issued in place of the jump smock: the Luftwaffe camouflaged field jacket, widely worn by other categories of Luftwaffe ground troops. In splinter camouflage, it had a large fall collar, shoulder straps, and either two or four pockets. Magazines for the StG44 assault rifle are carried in the pockets—the special triple pouches were in short supply. Note conventional hobnailed ankle boots. 5.FJD encountered the US 28th Div., and our man has clearly been plundering their transport.

H1: Jäger, 2.Fallschirmjäger-Division; France, 1944
The gradual disappearance of specifically paratroop items is more marked here, and this figure has features common to parachute troops on all fronts at this date. Some of the photos reproduced in this book show the use of the general issue helmet among units of paratroopers, here covered with both hessian and string netting. The 'water-pattern' smock displays the probably useless cloth 'holster' built into the right rear panel on many examples of the 'second pattern' smock. The trousers are the blue-grey general issue Luftwaffe type, confined by the canvas anklets which became common in 1943–45 as the laced ankle boot replaced the long marching boot throughout the Wehrmacht. The weapon is the effective 8.8cm RPzB 54 'bazooka'.

H2: Oberfeldwebel, Sturmgeschütz-Brigade XII Reichswald, January 1945
Apart from the integral SP gun units of parachute divisions, two brigades of assault artillery for independent operations under Corps or Army command were formed from Fallschirmjäger volunteers at Melun, France, in the first months of 1944, equipped with StuG III vehicles. In winter 1944–45 StuG-Bde.XI fought in support of 5.FJD on the southern flank of the Ardennes

offensive; it was heavily committed around Bastogne and fought the US 4th Armored Division, before being transferred to the Russian Front. After being heavily mauled in the Falaise Pocket in summer 1944 StuG-Bde.XII operated on the borders of Germany in support of 7.FJD and under 1.Fallschirmjäger Armee; the end of the war found the brigade at Cuxhaven under 2.Armee.

There are few photos of personnel of these brigades; but we take our figure from one of Ofw.Berndl of StuG-Bde.XII, who won the German Cross in Gold in the Reichswald fighting. He wears the field grey vehicle uniform of Army assault artillery, of a noticeably light shade to judge by the photo. Interestingly, his Luftwaffe rank patches are sewn to the collar complete with a small 'L'-shape of silver *Tresse*. His shoulder straps appear to be conventional blue-grey items from the Luftwaffe uniform, with normal ranking and *Waffenfarbe*. He wears the Iron Cross 1st Class, the Parachutist's Badge, and the Luftwaffe Ground Combat Badge — though not, it seems, the rare Luftwaffe Tank

Paratroopers photographed during the operations around the Arnhem corridor, September 1944: FJR 6 and 3. and 5.FJD all provided elements for these operations. These cheerful soldiers use two looted wheelbarrows to carry weapons, ammunition and a radio; they provide a good impression of the typical appearance of Fallschirmjäger in the final months of the war.(590/2333/7A)

Battle Badge instituted in November 1944. Conventional Luftwaffe headgear seem to have been worn with this uniform, including the paratrooper's helmet; and there was some use of camouflaged field jackets and jump smocks as combat dress.

H3: Unteroffizier, 9.Fallschirmjäger-Division; Eastern Front, 1945

Typical of the nominally airborne soldiers who fought as infantry in the last months of the war, this NCO wears no specifically paratroop items apart from his old green jump smock, which did survive in some cases even as late as this division's last battle before Berlin. The blue-grey 1943 *Einheitsfeldmütze* steadily replaced the sidecap as normal field headgear for all ranks from the middle of that year onwards. It bears conventional insignia; *H2* would also be wearing this headgear. The officers' version of this cap had silver piping around the crown seam. The collar of the *Fliegerbluse* is folded outside the smock to display the rank patches and *Tresse*. General issue Luftwaffe trousers are worn with marching boots, which are, surprisingly, quite common in photos of the last stages of the war. Leather items were often a mixture of Army black and Luftwaffe dark brown by this stage. The weapon is the Kar 43, a shortened version of the Gew 43 semi-automatic rifle, which used the same gas-operated system as the FG42.

Notes sur les planches en couleurs

A1 Vareuse, ancien modèle armée avec insigne de l'armée, portée avec équipement de parachutage complet. **A2** Le modèle ultérieur de parachute comportait un harnais différnet—remarquer le 'joug' cerrière les épaules. Le premier modèle de vareuse de l'armée de l'air. **A3** Uniforme journalière de sous-officier de la Luftwaffe, avec bande régimentale sur la manchette; les bandes de manchette n'ont été portées que quelques semaines après la déclaration de la guerre.

B1 L'officier ôte sa vareuse pour prendre son équipement qu'il remettra en place sur sa vareuse. L'équipement de saut est limité au pistolet, au masque à gaz porté sur la poitrine dans une sacoche, au bidon d'eau, à l'étui de cartes et c'est à peu près tout. **B2, B3** La vareuse a acquis des poches graduellement. Environ un homme sur quatre portait la mitraillette MP.40; quant aux autres, il leur fallait récupérer leurs fusils dans des containers largués séparément. Noter la cartouchière spéciale pour chargeurs passée autour du cou.

C1 Casques maintenant revêtus de toile camouflage ou vert uni. Remarquer les étuis de MP.40 attachés aux jambes pour le saut, et une dangereuse manière de porter la MP.40 sous le harnais, ce qui a certainement provoqué des blessures. **C2** Les photos représentent la veste de sauvetage portée ainsi de manière inefficace et dangereuse. Remarquer la MP.40 suspendu à la ceinture du harnais. Les vareuses camouflées apparaissent maintenant en grand nombre. **C3** Certains officiers portaient la tunique d'uniforme sous la vareuse au lieu de la Fliegerbluse. L'insigne de parachutiste qualifié, en textile ou en métal, se portait sur le sein gauche.

D1 Remarquer la position d'aterrissage balourde par suite de la fixation basse des cordes du parachute au harnais, et l'impossibilité de diriger le parachute en l'air. **D2** Soldat récupérant un fusil dans un container de charge de modèle standard dans la 'zone de largage'—de nombreux parachutistes furent tués dans l'île de Crète pendant qu'ils essayaient d'atteindre les containers dispersés. **D3** Quelques officiers de la campagne de Crète portaient la tunique tropicale de la Luftwaffe, complète avec l'insigne de collier. Le calot était la coiffure normale du Fallschirmjäger.

E1 L'uniforme tropical complet est porté ici avec la coiffure de service d'officier, version été à dessus blanc; remarquer la bande de manchette Luftwaffe de modèle ancien pour le théâtre des opérations d'Afrique. **E2** La coiffure 'Meyer' portée uniquement par les parachutistes et les hommes de la division 'Hermann Göring' était la même pour les officiers et les hommes de troupe. Remarquer les pattes d'épaules du modèle 'tropical'. **E3** L'écharpe et l'emblème de casque était particulier à la 1.Kompanie, I/FJR 5; d'autres unités les portaient en différentes couleurs. Noter le calot de type tropical.

F1 Uniforme de service d'un général, avec ses décorations des deux guerres mondiales. **F2** Version de parade inhabituelle de l'uniforme de bataille, avec les insignes et décorations ornant la vareuse; le harnais de parachute est porté sans le paquetage du parachute. **F3** Les campagnes d'Italie et de Sicile étaient souvent caractérisées par un mélange d'éléments d'uniformes tropicaux et européens. Noter le fusil FG.42 et la cartouchière spéciale.

G1 L'uniforme d'hiver de l'armée, capitonné, réversible gris/blanc était porté parfois par-dessus la vareuse et le pantalon de parachutiste. **G2** Version d'hiver de la coiffure M1943, et vêtement de camouflage blanc, mince, avec brassard temporaire, en couleurs, pour identifier l'unité. **G3** Certains 'parachutistes' n'avaient alors, guère sauté d'un avion; ils étaient utilisés uniquement comme fantassins; leurs uniformes et équipements devinrent mixtes, ne retenant que quelques éléments spéciaux des Fallschirmjäger.

H1 Cette arme est le lance-fusées anti-char de 8,8 cm RPzB 54. Noter le casque de fantassin avec revêtement serpillère. **H2** Un sous-officier de l'une des deux unités de canon d'assaut auto-moteur levée en 1944 parmi les parachutistes. L'uniforme normal desservant de canon d'assaut, auquel s'est ajouté les insignes de parachutiste. **H3** Trait typique des derniers mois de la guerre; la vareuse est restée mais les pantalons ordinaires et les bottes de marche remplacent les éléments spéciaux des parachutistes. La coiffure M1943 a remplacé le calot dès le milieu de 1943.

Farbtafeln

A1 Frühe Ausführung eines Armee-Kittels mit Insignien; er wurde mit voller Fallschirmausrüstung getragen. **A2** Spätere Ausführung eines Fallschirms mit unterschiedlichem Gurtwerk—beachten Sie den 'Bügel' hinter den Schultern. Erste Ausführung eines Luftwaffenkittels. **A3** Standard-Uniform eines Unteroffiziers der Luftwaffe mit Regiments-Manschetten; die Manschetten wurden bis einige Wochen nach Kriegsausbruch getragen.

B1 Offizier zieht seinen Kittel aus, um an seine Ausrüstung heranzukommen, die er anschliessend über dem Kittel trägt. Die Ausrüstung beim Springen bestand lediglich aus Pistole, Gasmaske in der Brusttasche, Wasserflasche, Kartentasche und wenig mehr. **B2/3** Mit der Zeit wurde der Kittel mit Taschen versehen. Nur einer von vier Männern hatte eine MP40, die anderen mussten sich die Gewehre aus den separat abgeworfenen Kanistern beschaffen. Beachten Sie den Patronengurt, der um den Hals hängt.

C1 Die Helme sind hier mit tarnfarbenem oder grünen Stoff bezogen. Die MP40-Tasche wurde vor dem Sprung am Bein festgebunden; eine MP40 unter dem Gurtwerk zu tragen, war gefährlich und hat sicherlich Verletzungen verursacht. **C2** Auf dem Foto sehen Sie, wie man die Schwimmweste trug—diese Art ist untauglich und gefährlich. Beachten Sie die MP40, die vom Gurt herunterhängt. Tarnfarbene Kittel werden hier schon massenweise getragen. **C3** Einige Offiziere trugen den Uniformrock anstelle der Fliegerbluse unter dem Kittel. Der Fallschirmjäger trug sein Rankabzeichen aus Stoff oder Metall auf der linken Brust.

D1 Ungünstige Landeposition wegen den zu tief angebrachten Fallschirmleinen am Gurtwerk. Während des Spunges lässt sich der Fallschirm nicht lenken. **D2** Soldat beschafft sich ein Gewehr aus einem Standard-Frachtcontainer in der 'Fall-Zone'—viele Männer sind auf Kreta bei dem Versuch, verstreute Container zu erreichen, ums Leben gekommen. **D3** Einige Offiziere der Luftwaffe auf Kreta trugen die Tropenausführung des Uniformrocks mit Kragenabzeichen. Das Schiffchen war die normale Kopfbekleidung der Fallschirmjäger.

E1 Hier die komplette Tropenuniform mit der weissen Sommerausführung der Offiziersmütze. Eine frühe Manschetten-Ausführung der Luftwaffe für Soldaten, die in Afrika dienten. **E2** Offiziere und Mannschaften der Fallschirmjäger sowie der Hermann-Göring-Division trugen diese 'Meyer'-Mütze. Beachten Sie die tropischen Schulterstücke. **E3** Das Schal und Helmabzeichen war für die 1. Kompanie, I/FJR 5, typisch. Andere Einheiten hatten Abzeichen in unterschiedlichen Farben. Beachten Sie die Tropenausführung des Schliffchens.

F1 Volle Dienstkleidung eines Generals mit Auszeichnungen aus beiden Weltkriegen. **F2** Ungewöhnliche Parade-Ausführung einer Felduniform mit Insignien und Auszeichnungen auf dem Kittel; Fallschirm Gurtwerk wurde ohne die Fallschirm-Verpackung getragen. **F3** Eine Mischung aus tropischer und europäischer Uniformteilen in Italien und Sizilien üblich. Beachten Sie das FG42-Gewehr und den besonderen Patronengurt.

G1 Die gepolsterte, wendbare grau-wiesse Winteruniform, die der Fallschirmjäger hier über Kittel und Hose trägt. **G2** Winterausführung der M1943-Mütze mit dünner, weisser Tarnkleidung und farbigen Armbinden, die vorübergehend zwecks Identifizierung der Einheit getragen wurden. **G3** Zu dieser Zeit waren nur wenige 'Fallschirmjäger' je gesprungen. Sie wurden als Infanterie eingesetzt und ihre Uniformen und Ausrüstungen wurden mi anderen vermischt, bis sie schliesslich kaum noch für Fallschirmjäger typische Eigenschaften hatten.

H1 Die Waffe: ein Panzerabwehr-Raketenwerfer RPzB54, 8,8 cm. Beachten Sie den Infanterie-Helm mit Sacküberzug. **H2** Ein Unteroffizier einer von zwei Sturmschutzeinheiten, die 1944 aus den Reihen der Fallschirmjäger entstanden. **H3** Für die letzten Kriegsmonate typisch: Kittel wurd weiterhin getragen, aber normale Hosen und Marschstiefel ersetzen die Spezialausrüstung der Fallschirmjäger. Die Feldmütze M1943 wurde seit Mitte 1943 anstelle des Schiffchens getragen.